Jack Beresford

An Olympian at war

JOHN BERESFORD

For River and Rowing
With best wishes,

John Beresford

First published in the United Kingdom in 2019 by
The Cloister House Press

ISBN 978-1-909465-87-9

Contents

Foreword

I have been moved to produce this book as a lasting memory of and tribute to my Father, Jack Beresford CBE. This is his story from schoolboy to infantry officer in the Line in 1918, to becoming one of the greatest oarsmen this country has ever known. This is the story he never wrote, which he had talked about writing for many years before his death.

The idea of focusing his story around his letters home from the front, came after watching Peter Jackson's remarkable film, **"They Shall Not Grow Old"**. By restoring, re-dubbing and re-colouring First World War footage Jackson erases the barriers of time, transforming soldiers of the First World War from remote black and white figures, to living, breathing men, enjoying their jokes, their football and sunshine during spells away from the battlefield. It seems to me that my 19-year-old father's 119 letters home to his parents, between April and October 1918 bring him and his comrades to life in the same transformative way with their keenly observed record of a soldier's daily experience of war and nature.

Jack survived the war and went on to became one of the most illustrious rowing champions in history, winning three Gold and two Silver medals in five consecutive Games from 1920 - a record not surpassed until the Sydney Games in 2000 when Sir Steve Redgrave won his fifth consecutive Olympic Gold.

The crowning moment of his rowing career came in the Double Sculls race during Hitler's Berlin Olympics in 1936.

Jack, aged 37 was competing with Dick Southwood, a studious-looking London jeweller, who was 30. They were old, the boat was out of date and there were suspicions of dirty tricks when their brand new lightweight boat was 'lost' in a railway siding near Berlin. Yet against the odds they won, causing Hitler to storm out of his box in fury.

It's tempting to think that the seeds of that victory - the determination, the optimism, the refusal to be bowed by odds - are all there to be seen in those youthful letters almost twenty years earlier.

My overriding feeling about them is that they portray both his love for his parents and care for his men. The constant worry that his parents suffered becomes apparent from his comments. One of his corporals (see letter No 102 of 03.09.18) says of him: *"One of the finest officers I've had in all my long experience in France. This isn't mere eyewash, I'm quite sincere."*

Between them Jack's Platoon won three Military Medals and one Distinguished Conduct Medal. Almost every man was wounded at least once with two becoming casualties four times and two men were killed in action or died of wounds. Jack did not escape uninjured. His letters come to an abrupt halt in October 1918, when he is wounded - but for the six months he was writing, his letters show the mixture of extremely long hard work often at night, excitement, fear, boredom, training, fun and relaxation that was an infantry officer's life.

A vivid story unfolds from Jack's letters as he arrives in France at the start of the German Spring Offensive of April 1918, which threatened to break through to the English Channel with disastrous consequences for the Allies. The story continues, showing the Allied build up to pushing the Germans back behind their 1914 Lines and the impact this had on the morale of both sides.

Jack Beresford 2/Lt, The Kings Liverpool Scottish Regiment,
November 1917

The letters are also revealing for what they do not say. Jack was writing to anxious loving parents and it is clear from a later letter, written to his daughter, that he was determined to shield them from the worst details of what he was confronting.

The book gives his life story in two parts.

Part One
Transcript of letters from the Western Front to his parents, with added points of historical interest in italics, followed by:

1.   A letter he wrote to his daughter, Pandora, shortly before his death, which sheds a slightly different light on his life in France.
2.   Souvenirs from the Front that he sent home. This passion for collecting nearly cost him his life, as one letter explains.
3.   Probable locations that he could not name because of the censor.

There is a palpable change in tone in Jack's letters as he is posted from

First letter home, 3rd April 1918

defensive positions to training for two weeks and in the last month before being wounded, to attacking and pushing back the German Front.

Part Two
His life before and after the war, including the story of his victory at the 1936 Berlin Olympic Games.

This section is based on an article by John Jenkins published in 2006 in The Journal of The Special Air Service entitled *"Rugby's Loss – Rowing's Gain"*.

With John Jenkins's agreement I have added further information, family reminiscences and photographs to his original work and divided the information under chapter headings.

John Beresford 2019.

Part One

Letters from the Western Front, Givenchy Sector, France, by the Jack Beresford, April to October 1918.

Liverpool Scottish platoon, Jack Beresford in centre. 1918

Additional paragraphs added to make reading easier, as letters generally fully filled the paper. Spelling and punctuation is unaltered from the original. Some notes of explanation are added in brackets in italics throughout the letters.

Platoon Commander Z Coy 1st/10th Battalion the Liverpool Scottish.
British Expeditionary Force (BEF), France.
Served in the Givenchy Sector of the Line.

1. 3rd April 1918. Hotel Folkestone.

I had a good journey down, arrived here just about 10. I have to report on the quay at 12:45, I think the boat sails at 2. Expect to be at Boulogne or Étappes for a least a fortnight so don't worry.

Thanks very much for coming to Victoria with me Dad, it would be a bit of a job with no one to help.

2. 3rd April 1918. G Infantry Base Depôt, BEF, France.

I had quite a good time at Folkestone, had ham and eggs for lunch at the Queen's. Went on board just after 1. Three transports went all together with destroyers, a submarine chaser and airships as escort. We had a fine passage over very calm. I saw some French torpedo boats and various other cargo boats all camouflaged, they looked weird.

Had veal and ham pie and ginger ale on board and when we landed had tea at the Cafe Maritime we left the port at 5 and went to where I am now in a motor lorry. 15 of us with our kit.

When we arrived it was drizzling slightly but as the camp is on sand hills it is very dry. I am in a tent with 3 other fellows in my regiment. Nearly all the French kiddies wear French army caps, they look funny little beggars. I have seen a lot of Chinese Labour Corps. They wear all sorts of weird kit, blue coats & whatever they can get hold of.

Will you please send me out 1 pair of pyjamas, my brogue shoes and my revolver pouch (on the washstand) as I find I shall need them after all.

I am in quite a comfortable mess and the tents have wooden floors. 2 beds of a type in my tent, we tossed for them and I won so I shall be very comfortable.

With best of luck to you all.
Your loving son,
Jack.

PS. I shall not be going into the line for a while, so don't worry.

3. 4th April 1918 BEF, France.

My dear Mother & Father,

I am going to number letters now as I don't think you are getting all of them, as I have written pretty well every day. I only marked that letter as urgent as I wanted it to get through quicker.

No thanks I don't need that kapok sleeping bag Dad dear, no papers either and I get plenty of chocolate out here. It is very good of you to think of all these things.

Uncle Pandy (*Also in 55th Division. Wounded in April.*) very likely did see me out with a party of Camerons, as I brought them up from the base to the line. When Pandy very likely did see me I was going from B to O I think.

I think you would laugh if you could see me now lying on my belly writing this letter. I am in a little post with 20 odd men and a couple of Sergeants

10

sleep in this shack with me. It is very warm in here. I don't even sleep with my trench coat on. All through the night we are very busy on the alert, wiring, digging, etc. Just before it gets light we camouflage our work in the shell holes as we are in a secret post & one of Jerry's planes would soon spot our post & soon we might get bumped a bit. As the last man comes into the shack he chucks loose earth on the path that has been trodden down. It is great sport. In the daytime we don't move from our positions, but sleep as much as possible. The game we are on is called 'baffling the Boche'. We have not started harassing the Hun yet. We had a fine Boche plane over today only a few hundred feet above us and he did not spot that we were in the old shack.

Well I hope you are not worrying about me as I am really very fit and well and having quite a good time. When I come back I shall have plenty to tell you and plenty to see at home I expect.

This last parcel I have sent off contains a German Very Light pistol. You have only to screw the barrel onto the body and it is fixed up, just one screw that is all. The two clips of cartridges in the German housewife have got the powder taken out of them.

I have not been able to get into a town locally to buy a present for Eric and granny and in all the villages round about when we get out on rest the villagers have cleared out the places.

Well the best of luck to you all I expect old Wink (*his younger brother*) is getting on well with his sculling.

Your loving son,
Jack.

4. 5th April 1918 **Officers Club. A.P.O. S17, France.**

My dear Mother & Father,

I have had very little to do today. My kit is now complete, I have got tin hat, equipment and ammunition, field dressing, cap comforter, etc so I'm ready now.

I went into the village this afternoon and did a little bargaining *(see below for souvenirs)*. I managed to get on in a fashion, at least I got what I want. French English and signs. It is a weird little place, broken down and dirty.

I had a great night's rest last night. I was very comfortable and warm I got into breakfast at 8:30 and reported at 10.

Well there is little else to say,

Except goodnight,
Jack.

5. 5ᵗʰ April 1918   BEF, France.

My dear Mother and Father,

Everything going fine here I received a parcel from Buzzards two days ago. It had a cake, a tin of shortcake and two slabs of chocolate in it. I don't know who it is from. I also received the chocolate from home, it was very welcome but I'd rather you didn't send it please.

Have been doing plenty of training here only just in the morning as it is very hot later on. We are getting quite good hands at bayonet fighting, at least my platoon is. I have got quite a fine crowd now and I seem to get on well with all the men in my lot.

Well there is nothing else at present.
Your loving son,
Jack.

6. 5ᵗʰ April 1918 BEF, France.

My dear Mother and Father,

Fritz has been a gentleman today he has only bumped us once or twice and the consequence is that we have all had a good sleep all day. Tonight I am going to have a wash in a shell hole, the first one since I came up here. I was out on patrol this morning with my sergeant but we did not see anything much.

I got bearings with my compass on to a pineapple (little minenwerfer) but that is all we did except to have a look at our belts of wire and see where they wanted repairing. So far I have not got any souvenirs, I brought in one of our rifles from in front but that is all.

I got your letter of the 30ᵗʰ last night Mother dear and was very glad to see it. You got a pretty good post that day didn't you. I thought you would think that German cigarette queer.

Well there is nothing else to tell you now I am afraid, except that we are having very quiet time.

I hope you're all fit and well.
Your loving son,
Jack.

7. 8th April 1918 1/10th Scottish KLR, BEF, France.

My dear Mother & Father,

I am very sorry I have not written you before but I have been on the move lately and I'm now 3 miles back from the line, which by the way is very quiet.

Well after being at the base from Wednesday to Friday afternoon 7 of us left for our battalion I was detailed to take a draft of 33 men of the Camerons & Scottish for our lot. We entrained at the base at 6:15 and arrived at ---------- at about 1 o'clock. There were crowds of troops on board. The train moved at 20 to 5 miles per hour, chiefly the latter, and the men were all in cattle trucks labelled 40 hommes ou 8 chevaux. The boys were running along on top of the train or sitting on the footplate, others were walking along beside train. One had plenty of time to get out, relieve nature, run on & get on board again. It was really a priceless sight. A lot of the boys got onto the engine tender and sat up there. The old Frenchman driving the train didn't know what to do.

When it got dark the boys all clambered in and went to sleep and when we arrived at ---------- I had quite a job to get them all out as they were so sleepy. On arrival we marched to the old French barracks and bed down. When I had got them all settled down I left to get to my old billet. It was The Railway Hotel and 4 of the others were already in & sleeping on the floor. I got in at 3 and it was 4 before I had settled down. 5 of us slept in a row. I just pulled my boots and puttees off also my tunic, put on my trench coat and got off to sleep as there were no blankets there (our valises were still in the train).

I got up at 10 then went off to the Officers Club and had breakfast after that a hot bath, then a shave. Then we had a look at the town. It was knocked about a good bit, no windows anywhere and plenty of houses down. I left at 2 with the draft for the reinforcement camp. We arrived about 3:30 and are still here.

Our mess is a dirty little estaminet *(A small cafe selling alcoholic drinks)* and after mess I and another fellow set off to get our valises from one billet where they had been put by mistake. We moved them off in an old wheel barrow, a weird contrivance and after much energy got them to our billet (an old farm). It was 20 minutes walk away and half the journey was along a bridle path ankle deep in mud. It was eleven o'clock before we got them settled down. I slept on the old stone floor in the kitchen, but I had my valise & blankets and was very warm and comfortable.

On Sunday morning we walked in to B-------- *(Bethune?)* about 5 ½ kilos away, I came back to lunch as I had to spend the afternoon censoring letters. I had a little shooting later on with my Cameron boys on the range.

Just before I left in the train from the base an old Black Watch sergeant who was once in the Scottish Horse and who I had spoken to earlier on came up

13

and gave me a knife as a present from "an old Scottish Horsemen". I thought it was awfully good of him.

I got 200 fags for my boys when we left base and 10 francs for them to get some buns etc, they were very bucked. They are all very fine boys, just 19 most of them, I only hope they get to my platoon later on. I don't know yet when I shall be in the line I expect I shall be a good time yet as I am not actually with my battalion.

One great thing about this country is the white bread and one great thing against it is dirt.

By the way have those two French caps arrived yet as I have not heard yet. My new address is at the top of the letter,

Well goodbye for the present, I am having a great time.

You're loving son,
Jack.

PS. All the farms here seem to have a filthy pool in the centre of the yards and the buildings all round in a square. Ours smells like a first rate London sewer but très healthy?
Mind you keep cheery and don't worry.

8. 10th April 1918 BEF, France.

My dear Mother and Father,

I really don't know what I can tell you as we have to be very careful. I could tell you all about the present scrap if I was allowed to, the Boche prisoners I have seen coming in and various other things. I am still a few miles behind the line and I'm not going up for a while yet. The place where I went to the other afternoon has had a good number of gas shells into it, where the postcards came from.

I went into ------- this afternoon with 3 other fellows. We caught a lorry going in had tea there and messed about a bit, caught a lorry and got back in time for mess.

I am having a great time here and enjoying myself very much. I have seen some very interesting things out here and we are giving the Old Boche a hell of a time, he has got it in the neck this time, at any rate here. Of course I don't know what is happening on either flank. You really know much less about the war in general here than at home as we seldom get papers and if you do they are 2 or 3 days old.

Well bon soir.
The best of luck to you all,
Jack

14

9. 13th April 1918 BEF, France.

My dear Mother and Father,

I have not joined my regiment yet, but on Thursday I went up with a platoon composed of the draft I took up. We went up and held the canal _____ (*letter 28 of 10th May 1918 says this was the La Basse canal, where on his 1st day in the line he was hit by a piece of, fortunately, spent shell*) (we were in reserve). We were put in an old breastwork. The Platoon on the right had one or two wounded. We were relieved at night and went back to billets in an old barn. I got some food at 11 that night. We were in all morning and I only got a few biscuits during the day, but I didn't feel hungry as it was quite good sport.

I will write you again soon but I'm very busy as have just moved.
Your loving son,
Jack.

10. Sunday 14th April 1918. BEF, France.

My dear Mother and Father,

Since last you got my letter I have moved again and now up with my battalion. Well last Friday I went off with a mixed battalion in reserve to the Highland Division. We had a great time as the weather was grand, plenty of food and nothing to do except lie in a field watching planes flying about. We came back from this about 6, found we had to move in a hurry so by 8 we were off. We reached the field where we were to bivouac for the night about 10 o'clock.

We were bombed on the way by some of Jerry's planes, but he did not get us and Archie (*anti-aircraft guns*) and some machine guns drove them off. It was a pretty sight watching the machine guns go for him as one in every five bullets they fire is luminous and the bullets look like a lot of stars going up for him.

When we got to our camp I managed to get a billet in a tent for the night. Bosch (*different spelling to his usual*) planes were busy for 2 or 3 hours over us, as they were trying to knock out a big gun that was firing near us.

On Saturday morning we left the canal again and moved off to my Battalion transfer lines, had some food there and then at 7 we left for the line. After an uneventful march we reached Battalion Headquarters. We lay on the road for 2 hours and shells came near us only twice. One beggar exploded and sent up lots of bricks, one which descended & hit me on the hip bone but I only just felt it. At this point we were only 400 yards from Jerry's line.

At 1 o'clock I took a ration party down to the ration dump to get the food for the batt. I finally dossed down at 2:30 in a little dugout made of concrete and elephant casing (very thick corrugated iron). Of the 7 officers that came up I was the only one that did not go up to the line (1ˢᵗ line trenches), so I was lucky as I managed to get a sleep. I have slept in my clothes for 3 nights now so I'm not doing so badly.

By the way you know Farrers old house by Workman's field, well that is the place I am at. We are having pretty cold weather again now but Friday was boiling hot. The little village where I am now does look a weird sight. It is well covered with shells holes and every cottage has been smashed to bits, most of the trees are smashed too.

I feel very sorry for the wretched refugees here. Heaps of them have been shelled out of their homes and are tramping back along the roads, wheeling prams and carts filled with their belongings. I saw a train load of them going back yesterday. Quite a lot of them were riding on the roof, they all seemed quite cheery.

So far I am having a very good time and our division has done awfully well. I expect you have seen it mentioned in the papers. Don't forget my address is now 1ˢᵗ/10 KLR, don't put 55ᵗʰ division. (*Both Divisions were in the Givenchy Sector*).

I got your first letter (Mother's) on Saturday that is all that has come through so far. I am glad you went down to the Club last Sunday for a row. I think of you having that row this morning while I am writing this letter in a dugout. Thanks very much for putting all my stuff away Mother dear.

Well good bye for the present.
Your loving son,
Jack.

11. Monday 15ᵗʰ April 1918. BEF, France.

My dear Mother and Father,

Yesterday the dugout I slept in was done in, a shell drove into the earth underneath it and exploded blowing the concrete floor up to the iron roof and wrecking all the wire netting beds except mine luckily. I was not in at the time. The old Hun shelled us with 5.9s and 8 inch continuously for 4 hours. One shell hit the remains of the house above & brought most of it down onto our dugout. We got covered with dust but that was all.

I was Duty last night at Batt H.Q. sat in a chair all night, it was a bit slow. I took the rum ration round to the boys in "McMahon's post" at 3:30 this morning. It was great stuff for warming you up.

I got to bed after breakfast this morning until nearly lunch time. The Hun started to shell us at 9:15, carried on till one when he eased up for half an hour to have his beer and sausage for lunch. At 1:30 he was off again. He is a dirty old swine.

This morning about 5 I saw a couple of our aeroplanes machine gunning the Boche. They turned Archies on them and machine guns firing luminous bullets. It was quite a pretty sight and very interesting.

You will be glad to hear that we are being relieved tonight. Motor buses are coming for us, that is we clear off out of the danger zone and then off into buses. I don't know what sort of rest we are to have but we ought to get at least 3 days. I am leaving a bit earlier tonight with another fellow to meet the buses and superintend the en-busing. Our batt is not quite three hundred any more. (*Indicates a lot of casualties*).

By the way have those two French caps come yet? I have got a French flying corps cap, a French respirator and a souvenir spoon to send home as soon as I get a chance to post them.

If you see anything in the papers about our gallant ally, the Porker Cheese (*Portuguese*), don't believe a word as they caused all the trouble here at this front. (*Overrun by the Germans in the Spring Offensive*).

I have just written a letter to old Bill Waldecker (*Old Bedfordian, who rowed with him at school*). The colonel of my Battalion out here is a great man. Was a Tommy first and won the Distinguished Conduct Medal then as an officer he got the Military Cross. He has got four wound stripes also plus another foreign decoration.

The Hun has made a mess of this part of the country. It is very flat and covered with small trees and fruit trees all of which are dead and smashed about very badly. The ground is covered with shell holes and especially the roads. Of the houses there are only one or two bits of walls left, the rest are just piles of bricks. On coming up to the village the first thing you see is a limber and one mule (dead) upside down in a shell hole in the middle of the road.

It is a weird noise hearing our heavy shells going along overhead. They sound just like big goods trains rumbling along at about 60mph, if you can imagine one doing that speed. The Boche crumps come with a whistle and hell of a bang and your hair sort of lifts on end for a second owing to the rush of wind and the ground fairly shivers. Then down come the stones and earth, that about describes them.

The little shells are nothing, they come whizz, bang, before you know where you are but the big ones you hear coming. This morning I saw a big shell hit a tree and cut it clean in half.

The other day a Boche came into one of the Scottish posts and gave himself up. He was smoking a cigar, saluted the sentry and said, "it's bon to be a prisoner, I was one in Russia before".

Thanks very much for your letter Dad dear, it was very welcome and came this morning. Are my letters being censored and have you guessed where I am? Tell me if so, as your letters are not censored.

Well goodbye for the present,
Your loving son,
Jack.

12. 18th April 1918 BEF, France.

My dear Mother and Father,

Thanks very much for the parcels, the chocolate was great but I get plenty over here and much cheaper, so I hope you won't send it. If there is anything I really want I will tell you.

Well I will tell you how I got on up in the line. I left the line about 7 o'clock in the evening when it was still light. I went off with another officer to see about motor buses to bring the battalion back to rest billets. Well when we left it was still light and we had to get down in ditches behind trees and take what cover we could as we got clear. The Old Boche was then only 400 yards away tried sniping at us but he did not get us. It was a bit of a sweat getting along as I had a trench coat on and also full fighting order (ie revolver, pack etc). We passed all sorts of curios, rifles, boots, shells all lying on the road, only I could not take anything back.

We got back pretty easily and found all the villages close to the line had been shelled to hell, the people had left everything behind them and lots of our boys were billeted in these houses with plenty of food all left behind.

It was about 12 o'clock before the battalion reached the point where the buses were waiting for them. At one o'clock we left in buses for rest billets behind the line. We arrived at 3 in the morning. We all had a good meal then off to bed. I got into bed at 7 and slept till 3 on Tuesday afternoon. Tuesday night we had a dinner with plenty of good champagne. It was a bon night.

Yesterday morning (Wednesday) we did nothing; in the afternoon we paraded in fighting order, when the commanding officer spoke to us and thanked us. Perhaps you have seen about it in the Papers, I wish you would keep anything that comes out about our division and date it, as I would like it for after the war.

I received another parcel of chocolate in a Gold Flake tin. I think it is Auntie Mabel's writing. There was nothing in it to say who it was from.

Well goodbye for the present,
Jack.

13. 21st April 1918 BEF, France.

My dear Mother and Father,

I got your letters this morning Mother dear, enclosing the cheque book. Am glad everything is going well.

We have moved forward a bit again and are now waiting to go up in reserve, expect to be out of the line for 2 or 3 more days yet.

Everything is going very well out here at present and the Boche has had tremendous casualties on his front. In the last show our battalion is reckoned to have killed between 500 and 800. It was a weird site to see our boys in the line wearing German greatcoats as we went up without overcoats and it was a bit cold at night.

Well there is no more news now except that the general commanding the division spoke to us yesterday and thanked us for the fine show we had just made. Also that we had killed crowds of Boches but there were still plenty more to kill (this means the line again shortly).

Well so far I am having a great time, one big slack.
Well cheerio,
Jack.

14. 22nd April 1918 BEF, France.

My dear Mother and Father,

I am now in a new place again, up in support in a nice snug little cellar. Nothing doing here so far, in fact a good rest cure.

I have sent off a parcel with Boche cap in it, French respirator, French flying corps cap, Boche bullets, a piece of shell that hit me without affect and a revolver. I doubt if the parcel will reach you but I am chancing it. Up here I have just snaffled a Boche Very Light pistol, also a fine fuse cap. There are endless souvenirs out here if you can only carry them.

Thank Eric for his letter and tell him he can do what he likes with my autograph book. Uncle Pandy is jolly lucky I think.

On Saturday we moved up in buses from rest billets to nearer the line. It was a grand day and the country looked a treat. I slept the night in a shack made of tarred felt, v comfortable. By the way for supper that night had 4 eggs and a half pound of steak.

On Sunday after being spoken to by our brigadier and congratulated concerning the last battle we were in, I moved off to take over my company's sector in the support line. It was ten kilos away in full marching order and very hot day. Our company is in little bits of trench & shell holes, but we are very comfortable.

Well cheerio for the present.
I will write again when I get a chance.
Jack.

15. 23rd April 1918   BEF, France.

My dear Mother and Father,

I am on a fairly busy job at night, but nothing doing in the daytime. On Sunday night I was out with a working party digging a trench from midnight to 4 in the morning. We had one near shave only; as we were going along the road the Boche suddenly plunked a shell in the field about 8 yards away. It was quite fun to see that party disappear, in a second or two they had faded into shell holes or ditches by the road. I got down in a ditch, it was lucky I did as a Whizzbang landed within 2 yards of me, but I was well down & out of the way. Jerry only strafed the road for about 5 minutes & then stopped. He does it in the hope of catching ration parties.

Don't you worry if you see any rot in the papers about old Fritz whacking us, as we have absolutely got him, especially on this front where he has had a devil of a strafing so far.

Well I hope everything is going OK at home. Are the fowls keeping it up well? Remember me to Uncle Pandy and also he might be able to tell you something about my division, as he was in it.

Well goodbye,
Jack.

16. 24th April 1918   BEF, France.

My dear Mother & Father,

Well things are still going strong here & we are pretty busy. Last night I was again out with a working party of 25 men digging trenches from 9.15 to 12.15.

This morning one platoon of our coy & another coy carried out a stunt on the Boche. We went up & recaptured a keep that Uncle Pandy's regiment had lost and could not retake. Our boys did it though, this is the second time. It was at the same old place where I was 10 days or so back next to "Workman's Garden".

We have captured three machine guns and done in a lot of the blighters 202nd Reserve Infanterie Regt of the 4th German army. One Boche that gave himself up, came in and said to one of our fellows "good morning Jock" he promptly got his backside booted by one of our sergeants. About 100 Boche were killed altogether.

Well good night now, this time I am not going out tonight & hope to get a decent rest instead.

I hope you are all very fit and well and are not worrying.
Your loving son,
Jack.

17.   24th April 1918   BEF, France.

This is a German letter card that came from the keep we captured this morning its name is Route A Keep but I cannot tell you where it is. Although I expect the papers will have full particulars of the attack and also tell you where about's it is. I was not in the attack. (*See Letter 28, 10th May 1918*).

Jack.

18.   25th April 1918   BEF, France.

My dear Mother and Father,

Just a line to let you know I am still fit and well. Am going down for a rest in a day or two I think.

I heard today that poor old Thurlow had 6 machine gun bullets through the head. At present I am second in command of my company, that is Z company, 50 men and 2 officers.

Well cheerio,
Jack.

19. 26th April 1918 BEF, France.

My dear Mother & Father,

We have moved to another part of the line again. We are about 1 mile further on. We got up here about 1AM this morning and settled down in a fashion. We are in the middle of a big wood by a big canal. The ground is very waterlogged as the Boche has hit the canal bank once or twice and flooded the country a bit. We are living in a keep, it is a big breastwork and in jolly good repair. It is quite a peaceful spot and this morning I heard a cuckoo.

I went out on the scrounge this morning and got a Boche tin hat. I doubt if I shall be able to get it home but when we come out of the line I shall take it with me if I can.

This morning I had breakfast at 6:30 then turned in at about 8, got up for lunch and went off with a runner to find the company on our left and get in touch with them. The country is all swamps and ditches with rank grass nearly up to your waist in parts. We were out for a couple of hours, it was quite a change being able to get some exercise. By the way I also won a canvas bucket and after tea I propose, the Boche permitting, to have a wash.

Some more Boche prisoners have just come through from another battalion that has just been stunting. We have got them on the hop here and the best of it is that the 1st German Guards reserve division is now in front of us. He has been for the last 2 days now and has had a thin time of it too. The prisoners that we have taken in the last day or two all say they are fed up with the war and it is only the higher command that makes then keep on with it.

Let me know when any parcels I send back get through will you please. I was very glad to get your letter of the 20th Dad dear and to hear the news.

When uncle Pandy was wounded was it on the 9th at Gorre Brewery?

Lately have you been getting a letter from me regularly every day, as I have been writing each day.

Nothing to report, situation quiet.
Your loving son,
Jack.

20. 27th April 1918 BEF, France.

My dear Mother and Father,

I've got a funny story for you this time it is absolutely true and happened in a place called Cailloux Keep. My company commander was going round the trenches just after "stand to" when he came across Sergeant MacCormack grumbling to himself. He was saying "it's not fair, it damn well's not fair". So Mr Lewis asked him what was the matter, so he said, "there's been a fellow hopping about our line in a German cap and I had 10 shots at him and missed him every time". Then it turned out that it was Sergeant Craig. So Mr Lewis went and saw Craig who said he did it for sport and that every time old MacCormack got his rifle up to site on him he bobbed down. Old Craig is one of the maddest chaps in the battalion out here.

This is another true yarn. Down at Épehy (the Boche has it now) *(between Cambrai & Saint Quentin, just west of the now A26)* the trenches are full of frogs and two men are detailed from each company to collect frogs and put them in sandbags, tie the bag up, and throw them away. One fellow known as 'Frog King' used to bayonet them and when he had got about 20 on his bayonet, used to pull them off into the sand bag.

Today has been uneventful, but tonight is très bon as we are being relieved and going back for a week's rest. We leave via a bridge over the canal called Waterloo Bridge, a little further up are Westminster and Vauxhall Bridges. Piccadilly Circus, Caledonian Road, Harley Street and a lot of other old friends are round about here.

Today some of our fellows on the canal have been pulling in roach. When a shell bursts in the canal and stuns the fish in a big area of water, you can haul in the fish when they come to the top. So our fellows in the post by the canal had fried roach for lunch. In this canal you are not allowed to drop a bomb as, there are cables laid in the bottom, but in a lot of canals you get plenty of fish by that way of fishing; tell Uncle George when I come back on leave I will bring a few for his use if he likes, you are dead sure of getting something. Well I don't think there is much more to tell you.

Well I am now going to get 40 winks before marching back to rest billet.

By the way this morning a Boche plane with our markings on it, machine gunned us this afternoon, but it very soon hooked it.

In this wood there are plenty of mauve violets growing.

Well I hope you are all fit and well.
Your loving son,
Jack.

PS. I have been sleeping very comfortably up here on an old frame with canvas over it. I pull my feet into a sandbag, one foot in a bag, they keep your legs and knees fine and warm. I put my trench coat over my body, tin hat as a pillow and cap comforter on my head and there I am.

21. 28th April 1918 BEF, France.

My dear Mother and Father,

I arrived in rest billets about 3 o'clock this morning after a bit of a march. Had a bath this evening and feel a different man now.

I have got another German cap now (the 3rd) belonging to the Prussian Guards, it was taken in the last show; a German Bible called the Christian soldier, in it is a picture of Christ and behind him a burning cottage; two shoulder straps of the 201st regiment; some German tobacco.

Well good night.
I will write a decent letter soon,
Jack

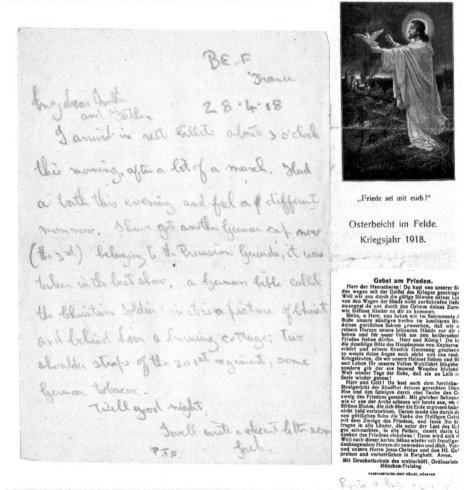

Picture of Christ from a card inside a Prussian Guard bible. Letter 28th April 2018

P.T.O

Thanks very much for last letter, Vera *(sister)*. Also one from you Mother dear. Excuse me not writing anymore. I am very tired.

22. 1ˢᵗ May 1918 BEF, France.

My dear Mother and Father,

I am very sorry I have not written to you lately but now that I am out in rest billets I find it much harder to find time to settle down and write a letter.

Well I came out at 3 on Sunday morning we had a 6 miles march back and arrived in a place where there were a few huge guns that kept us awake for awhile. As the place got too hot we moved on to another place the following day.

I got your letter of the 25ᵗʰ on the 29ᵗʰ and I received the parcel with pyjamas in it etc nearly a fortnight ago. I did say I had received it. You evidently could not have received these letters. I sent a parcel back about a week ago, please let me know when it arrives as I have another ready to send if it gets back.

We had quite a good little dinner last night at an éstaminet in the village and after that slept in a hut where the Chinese Labour Corps used to live. I told you about them climbing trees and telegraph poles if a shell burst near them didn't I.

While I am out of the line there is absolutely nothing to tell you. I am very fit and well and I'm doing alright everything is going strong and the Boche seems very fed up with it in this area at least. The rain also has helped to put the cap on Fritz now.

Well goodbye for the present. I am awfully glad the garden is going on so well and also that you like the photo. When I get a chance to get something for Granny and Eric I will.

Your loving son,
Jack.

23. 1ˢᵗ May 1918 BEF, France.

My dear Mother and Father,

Have done nothing today except reorganise the two battalions into one (*because of the general manpower crisis*). I have stuck to the battalion but quite a lot have gone back to other divisions.

The weather is dull and cold. Am having a very good time.

We had a dinner last night. 12 bottles of Heidseck for 9 of us and 3 champagne cocktails each. I've a bit of a thirst this morning. Well shall be sending another parcel home in a day or two.

Your loving son,
Jack.

24. 3ʳᵈ May 1918 BEF, France.

My dear Mother and Father,

Just a line to let you know that everything is OK with me. I came up to the line last night and am back in the same place as on 12ᵗʰ of last month when I first joined the batt. I sent a parcel of things off before I came up. I wonder whether they will reach home.

Please excuse the awful scrawl but I am now baffling the Boche and living in a tiny shack called a little elephant. Two sergeants live in here with me, it is only 3 to 4 feet high: 10 feet long, 5 feet wide, but is fine & cosy. The men live in another one just by me and the Lewis gunners in another. In case of attack we occupy shell holes.

The Boche is about 400 yards away in daytime, 200 at night when we can hear him cough or talk. So far it is good sport but a bit stuffy as in daytime we can't show our noses outside (we sleep all day and come out at night). We live on bully Maconochies and biscuit. (*The main staple in the trenches was corned beef, or bully beef: cooked, preserved, tinned meat, chiefly from Argentina. The other tinned staple was "Maconochie" - a pork and beans meal, named after the Aberdeen-based manufacturer*).

Well goodnight.
Your loving son,
Jack.

25. 7ᵗʰ May 1918 BEF, France.

My dear Mother and Father,

I am out of the front line now and am back in support. We are doing a 12 days spell. Weather is pretty bad. Coming back early this morning from the line was very bad. No moon, pitch dark, a few shells and tons of shell holes. I was mud from head to foot. Having to lead the way meant plenty of "don't go down the mine Daddy" and I did quite a few times, mud and water to my knees.

I was the first to get my platoon back, we got some tea then bedded down. Will send a long letter tomorrow only am just off up the line with a wiring party. Today I got up at 3 this afternoon, had a bath in a biscuit tin.

Good night,
Jack.

26. 8th May 1918 BEF, France.

My dear Mother and Father,

We were relieved at 1 in the morning on the 7th and started off to march back to the point where guides were to pick us up and lead me and my Platoon back to reserve breastwork. Well we could not find any guides so we started off on our own. It was pouring with rain and was pitch dark (by the way we came back from Farrars House). You could hardly keep to the track owing to the shell holes. I arrived at the new place at 3:30 and was covered with mud from head to foot as I had fallen into a good many shell holes on the way.

As soon as my boys were bedded down I got off to my corner and slept till 3 in the afternoon, then had breakfast after that a bath in a biscuit tin and I felt fine.

We are doing a 12 days spell in the line, 4 days in advanced posts (that means next to Jerry), 4 days in reserve then 4 days in the front line again after that rest (with luck).

At 8 p.m. I had to leave for the line again. Well I missed my way and nearly walked into the German line. I just struck an advanced post, otherwise I should by now have been a prisoner. It was pitch dark and the mud very bad. In one part I had to go for nearly a quarter mile across marsh land and then another part I went just to the top of my hose tops in mud. Finally I went into a ditch up to my waist in mud and water, but it soon dried.

I got to the party I had to take wiring about 11 o'clock and finished by 2 and were back home by 4 a.m. When we got back there was plenty of fine hot porridge which made a great difference to us all. I was in bed by 5 and up again at 8. I had a wash by the canal, it took me till 9.15 before I had finished, then I had some breakfast.

This evening I went out on the canal in a homemade Rob Roy *(kayak type of canoe)* it was great sport. After that three of us stripped and had a swim in the canal, the water was grand and warm and it was topping swimming about in the water. The weather has been so grand and hot that we have been wandering about in our shirts all today.

Things are getting very lively here again now. We have had Jerry's planes right back here over us and one flew along just above us. They didn't care a damn and our Lewis anti- aircraft gun put a good many holes through his plane but the machine was not brought down.

By the way I didn't tell you did I that our divisional general told us that we are "the most hated division in the British Army" according to the Germans. General Kentish told me today to remember him to Uncle Pandy.

Well I'm back in the same topping wood that I wrote to you about 10 days ago. I received an awfully nice letter from Auntie Mabel this morning. I was very bucked to get it.

Well good night, I am going to have a bon sleep tonight <u>with luck</u>. I am feeling very fit & well and am enjoying myself very much.

Well cheerio.
Your loving son,
Jack.

27.   9th May 1918 BEF, France.

My dear Mother and Father,

I am having a ripping time here now the weather is perfectly great, it is boiling hot, as hot as the hottest days of summer at home.

I had a grand wash in the canal after breakfast. As I was washing a Hun plane came over very low. All the guns got on to him but he was untouched. He flew around here and went back towards his line. Later he came over again, got turned back and finally crashed in flames in our front line.

You have nothing to worry about for a good while yet even if funny things do happen. My present company commander is named Dickinson he rowed for Pembroke College, Cambridge and remembers you. He said to me that he used to like watching you race more than any other man (*Jack's father, "Berry" Beresford won a silver medal in the IV at Stockholm Olympics, 1912 amongst other notable successes*). He is a damn nice fellow.

Good night,
Jack.

28.   10th May 1918 BEF, France.

My dear Mother and Father,

I am afraid yesterday's letter was a bit of a hurriedly finished one but we expected a stunt and I had to finish in a hurry and get away to my position. However it all ended alright and Fritz got a terrific strafing he did not give us anything in return baring a few gas shells but the gas was so slight that we did not even have to wear our masks, it just makes your eyes water a bit.

I slept in the bottom of a trench all night had my trench coat on and an oil sheet (waterproof groundsheet) wrapped around me, a woollen cap on my head and tin hat for a pillow; have to sleep in full equipment with gas mask on your chest ready to put on. It is funny how quickly you get into the way of sleeping anywhere like that.

Lately the Hun has had a hell of a time from us. We blew up 12 out of 19 dumps (of ammunition, bombs etc) in this sector. Also 25 out of 50 guns were knocked out in 2 days, that rather did his push in. We should have a quiet time again now he has had more than enough of it lately.

Thanks very much for your letters of the 5th Mother dear. I am glad that parcel came alright. That would be a good idea having those caps cleaned but before they go would you take the buttons off the front so as to sow on when they come back. The red white and black is always on top and the badge of the German army. The black and white one is of the state of Prussia. Each state has a different coloured button. Bavaria is red and black etc.

In that parcel that came the bullets are Germans, that piece of shell hit me the first day in the line on the La Bassée canal *(not censored, confirms his location)*, it was spent though.

I am awfully pleased to get all the letters I do from you. I get one about every day and I hope you do. I was very pleased to get your long letter of the 5th Dad dear it is great getting those German glasses for me Dad dear, thanks very much, but I would rather they stayed at home as a curio. How did you get them.

You say do I like your scrawls. You bet I do. And I don't want any socks yet thanks. Did a souvenir spoon of B------- *(Bethune?)* arrive in that parcel. You don't say so, if so it is for you Mother dear.

I am glad Wink *(Eric, brother)* is keen on sculling now. That is wrong about addressing a first or second lieutenant as Mr so and so on an envelope. You speak about him as Mr so and so.

In that picture I sent you, do you notice the burning cottage in the background? There is nothing I want sending out thanks.

Many happy returns of the day Mother dear from the line. I will try and get something when I come out for a bit. I am going up to the front line tonight for 4 days. Am in the 3rd line now.

Had a grand bathe in the canal yesterday afternoon. It was topping and so peaceful, you would hardly realise there was a war on. Last night yes, much war on. Very quiet today and much colder no sun, fairly misty. Didn't bathe today but had a wash in the canal.

All those German souvenirs sent back were from a famous place called Route A Keep *(see below here)*. It doesn't matter me telling you now as we have blown it to hell and it exists no more. When the next dispatch comes out you may see something about it.

Jack Beresford wearing gas mask & kilt apron. 1917

- ROUTE A KEEP, near Gorre.

(The following is taken from a post on 1ˢᵗ August 2008 to the Great War Forum by Ian Riley).

Using the maps from Coop's story of the 55th (West Lancashire) Division, scaled by trial and improvement to the Série Bleue 1:25000 map, I think that Route A Keep is at:
50°32'56.51"N   2°43'25.71"E   using Google Earth. This has given good results for other locations in the area.

The track plan is almost the same today as on Coop's maps, based on trench maps.

Take the road from Festubert towards the Post Office Rifles Cemetery. About 100m beyond the cemetery take the track on the right. If I remember, we drove up to a large farm (looking like the Bates Motel), about 400 metres, dumped the car and walked 300 metres or so further north to the four way track junction. I think Route A Keep was in the NW quadrant. I cannot recall seeing any concrete emplacements but looking at Google Earth there seems something suspicious immediately to the SE of the four way track junction. 50°32'55.76"N 2°43'26.81"E. If I recall it is quite overgrown but it is two or three years since I was there.

29. 11ᵗʰ May 1918 BEF, France.

My dear Mother and Father,

Just a line to let you know that I am fit and well was out on patrol this morning, came across a dead Boche, found an iron cross ribbon of the 1st class on him, took a few buttons, his shoulder strap and identification disc. He belonged to the 362ⁿᵈ Jaeger regiment, enclosed is ribbon. (*See letter 102 when he said he had a close shave with corporal Chadwick whilst taking this 'souvenir'*).

Am living in an old cellar, quite a good shack, only 2 or 3 inches of water on the floor.

Best of luck,
Jack

30. 12ᵗʰ May 1918 BEF, France.

My dear Mother and Father,

I received your letter and parcel of chocolate. The chocolate was grand, the best I have tasted, but please don't send as I know how difficult it is to get at home and out here there is plenty.

I am glad the parcel I sent arrived alright. Those German cartridges have had the powder taken out, they are absolutely safe. You could chuck them in the fire and nothing would happen. That big pistol is a German Very Light pistol (he sends his star lights up from that). The little black book is a German bible and there is a German housewife there. So now you know what they all are. Perhaps Wink would like to clean the pistol up a bit.

Well I am afraid there is nothing to tell you at present, although when I come out I will let you know a bit more about it. We are doing 4 days up the line now that will make a 12 day spell altogether.

I am very comfortable now except for the smell and this place is rather like a London sewer.

I got that letter from Mrs Thurlow she wants to know all particulars so I shall tell her it all. I am sorry for her. I was going to write but I did not know how to tackle it, I didn't think she would be so plucky and wish to know it all.

I hope you are all well.
Your loving son,
Jack

31. 13th May 1918 BEF, France.

My dear Mother and Father,

Things are going alright here but it is a bit cold although the rum keeps you alright. It is wonderful the difference it makes to us here. Stand-to the whole night and it gets cold then at about 3 A.M. I take the rum round and the fellows are all lively and ready for anything.

I was out on patrol this morning from 2:30 to 4 with a corporal and 2 men. Did not come across anybody. I brought in a German rifle that was all. There were crowds of German dead out there and the stink was pretty rich. It is a true enough saying you can smell a German, he stinks twice as much as our fellows do. I suppose it is the sausages and black bread he gets.

Shall be in rest, so cheer up. I am very fit and well and we are having good sport, the old Hun doesn't like us.

I am afraid this is a rotten sort of letter but I can't tell you anything yet. I hope you are getting better Dad dear, I am sorry you are so rotten. Do chuck that Specials job and look after yourself.

Your loving son,
Jack.

32. 15th May 1918 BEF, France.

My dear Mother and Father,

Am now out of the line and in comfortable rest billets, very well and dead tired. Will write a decent letter tomorrow and going to turn in early, will be out of the line for 6 days.

I got your letter of the 10th today, am sorry to hear that Dad is so rotten. Why can't he take a good rest and be careful of himself. It does seem madness. It worries me to think you are like that.

Well I'm very fit and content will be sending a German pack and one or two other things back in a day or two. I got them all on patrol this last time.

Well goodnight.
Your loving son,
Jack.

33.   15th May 1918 BEF, France.

My dear Mother and Father,

I am afraid that again it is only a scratchy letter but we get up at 3:45, parade from 5 to 8, breakfast at 8, go to bed from 8:30 to 12:30. Lunch at 1. Then I had to go up to reconnoitre position about 14 miles there and back, weather boiling. Arrived back at 7, had dinner, went to bed at 9:30 till 3:45.

Am very glad to hear Dad is going away for a rest, he must be very bad or I know he would not go. You must be rotten too, Mother dear. I do hope you will both go away for a spell, I am sure you both need it very badly.

Well perhaps tomorrow I will be able to give you a proper letter.

Have you got that letter yet with the Iron Cross ribbon in it, as I rather value it.

Well goodnight.
Your loving son,
Jack.

PS. I am still very fit and well but frightfully sleepy.

34.   16th May 1918 Whit Sunday, France.

My dear old Dad,

I was awfully pleased to get your two letters this afternoon from Hastings. I do hope you get really well again and that you will take things lightly.

At last I am beginning to realise what tiredness is. This last time I had quite a fair dose of it. ** Patrolling solidly for 8 hours without an easy and on a frontage of 250 yards. We had little posts out and 25 men to hold it. It was more nervy than anything but it didn't take long to settle down. Of course we were all armed pretty well with bombs etc. I always carried a rifle and bayonet and a bomb in each pocket. **

** This part **. *See below.*

I am grand and fit now, the weather is wonderful, I get a cold shower every evening. The big town nearby is burning away merrily. I am still in the old sector.

We go about in shirt sleeves all day here, it is really topping. Last night I went to a concert got up by our battalion. It was topping and is wonderful the difference it makes to the fellows.

I am sending another parcel back, it is a German pack made of cow skin, a German gas mask, German water bottle, small German bayonet (it would look fine if it could be repainted. The old paint remains on it in places so that it would be easy to mix the colours correctly), some German buttons (the ones with the crown on and one with No 11 on it), the others are French. There are two small German fuse caps, they are quite safe, nothing to go off in them. Some German tobacco, I think it is a substitute, a little round tin with pepper in it. This parcel of things all came back from various men in the 362nd regiment, 4th Ersarz Division in their attack on the 9th April. Oh the pack came from a private of the 1st Guards reserve regiment.

Well I hope you get well quickly.
Your loving son,
Jack.

P.S Please tell Mother nothing about my last do in the line, ** to **. The rest I am telling her.

35. 16th May 1918 BEF, France.

My dear Mother and Father,

I had a fairly good doing the last time up and am very glad to be back in rest for a bit. I had a couple of shots at 2 unwily Huns, I downed one but not the other.

I am very fit again now after a good sleep but at the time the last go up the line rather told on me as I had a line to hold of 250 yards with 25 men counting myself and I was out patrolling in front from 9 till 4 a.m. every night.

We used to sleep a bit during the day but had to be very careful, especially one day when he gave us a bit of gas, minnies and 5.9's. I can assure you it's not very pleasant to be covered with mud and stones thrown up from his bursting shells. Some "leave trains" (14 inch shells) also came over just in rear of us. The holes they make are so big that you could get the stables inside easily, that is if you take off the part where the horse stalls are. The strafe was because we annoyed him a little to the south.

Today most of our fellows are wandering about in kilt aprons only, so you can guess how hot it is.

I maybe out of the line for a little while this time.

Well I hope you are both get better quickly.
Your loving son,
Jack.

PS. £1 birthday present Mother dear and many happy returns of the day.
    5/- each for Eric & Vera's birthday.

36. 19th May 1918 BEF, France.

My dear Mother,

Can't you managed to get away for only a week even. I'm sure it would do Dad a lot more good if you were there and I know it would buck you up a lot, I am sure you need it.

Well I am having a topping time here now the weather is boiling and we do nothing but sit about in our shirt sleeves and drink lime juice. Last night I went to a fine concert. This morning I went to a Presbyterian service.

I'm sending another parcel home, everything is absolutely safe in it. The fuse caps included. The following are in it, a German pack I got from a German in the 1st Guards reserve regiment. The other things came from various men in the 362nd regiment 4th Ersatz Division. There is a German gas mask, 2 fuse caps from German shells, a small German bayonet, water bottle, tin filled with German 'baccy, German tin with pepper in it, in that are also some buttons, the ones with a crown on and one with No 11 are German, the others are French, I think that is all it contained.

Well I hope you are all very well and happy.
Your loving son,
Jack.

37. 20th May 1918 BEF.

My dear Mother and Father,

Have done nothing today except one or two parades. This afternoon my valise was packed up as we are moving tonight. I have been left out of the line this time, as we have one or two buckshee officers. Two of us are staying out and the other two officers are going up instead, so you won't be able to worry for 16 more days now.

Well that is all the news. I expect from your point of view it is very good. The weather is frightfully hot we still go about in shirtsleeves.

Your loving son,
Jack.

38. 21st May 1918 BEF, France.

My dear Mother,

I got 3 letters today, one from Dad and 2 from you, I am very bucked. But I am very sorry you have missed those letters for such a while as I try to get a letter or card back each night. Have you got that Iron Cross ribbon yet?

Well this morning I had a busy time of it. I was out of bed at 3:30 left at 4 on a working party and got back at 10. We had only arrived in here at 11 last night from our rest billets. I am staying out of the Line this time for 12 days I think and then the batt comes out for 6 days so that makes 18 days.

Well now you can rest in peace for a good while.
Your loving son,
Jack.

The Lily of the Valley is from a burning town, the big one here. He has done it in now, he is a swine. I was in there two days ago just to see the flames. It was a great sight and piles of smoke going up. The town stinks of mustard gas.

39. 22nd May 1918 BEF.

My dear Mother,

Just a line to let you know I am still fit and well. I have been on a Lewis gun course this morning. The weather still very hot, I am getting very red faced now and enjoying myself very much.

I hope you are very well Mother dear.
Your loving son,
Jack.

40. 23rd May 1918 BEF, France.

My dear Mother and Father,

Yesterday I had a bathe in the stream just by, it was topping, as you get so filthy round the legs in a kilt.

In the evening I fired a 6 inch howitzer. It is wonderfully simple. You just pull the lanyard that fires an ordinary blank cartridge. This sets the charge off which sends away the shell. We lifted the shell up and rammed it into the gun and fired it off. The flash it makes is pretty hefty, you hardly know where you are for the second.

Last night we pulled our beds out into a field and slept outside for the night, it was topping. I felt grand and fit when I woke up in the morning. We got up and went down in our pyjamas to a stream nearby where we had a bathe, then came back, dressed and had breakfast. After breakfast we carried on with the Lewis gun course.

Yesterday evening we were all wandering about in kilt aprons as it was so frightfully hot, most of the men were going about in just their shirts while in camp.

It has suddenly turned very cold again & is very cloudy. I think we are going to get a good deal of rain. I am enjoying myself very much, it is a great time we are having.

I hope you are all very well.
Your loving son, Jack.

41. 24th May 1918 BEF, France.

My dear Mother and Father,

I was out on a working party early this morning. I was up at 3:30 and left here at 4, didn't get back here until 12:45. It was pretty thick, especially as after an hour it started to pour and kept it up the whole time we were there. We got soaked through but it didn't worry the men much, they cheered right up when we got home. I had some food, then got straight to bed. I got up at 5 o'clock to write this and have tea.

I am feeling very fit and well now as I have got my trews on and have changed my dirty things.

Love, Jack.

42. 25th May 1918 BEF, France.

My dear old Dad,

I am glad the weather is so topping for you Dad dear, it will do you a lot of good. It is just on the hot side out here even with a kilt. I should think it must be awful in trousers, as you see we can wear kilt aprons only.

I have been out in a field all the morning on a Lewis gun course, it was very hot but rather nice, I am getting pretty red-faced now. We are having a grand time here, it is quite nice and peaceful and we have very little to do here so far as the wind has died down considerably.

Well I am sorry to say there is nothing more.
Your loving son,
Jack.

43. 25th May 1918 BEF, France.

My dear Mother and Father,

I have been doing absolutely nothing today except have a rest. During the morning I was on a Lewis gun course and this afternoon I have been censoring letters. Last night I got to bed early and had a good sleep, have now slept off the effects of yesterday's working parties and felt quite fit again.

I got both your letters yesterday Dad dear of the 16th and 19th. You seem to have had a great time with the fish, it must have been great sport.

At present I am billeted in an estaminet, there is no liquor in though. Four of us sleep on wire beds in the bar, as it is also our mess we are very comfortable.

The weather is quite good again today and I think we have got rid of the rain for a bit.

I'm afraid there is absolutely no news now, the old Boche is absolutely whacked now and I expect on our arms.

Well I hope you will go down with Dad for a rest Mother dear, I am sure it would do him more good and I know it would do you more good than sitting at home worrying, when there is nothing to bother about.

I hope you are all well at home.
Your loving son,
Jack.

44. 26th May 1918 BEF, France.

My dear Mother and Father,

I was very pleased to get your letter Mother dear. I am glad the present came in useful, also I meant you to have the souvenir spoon. I bet the front garden looks topping now with all the geraniums in and I am glad you are going down to Hastings. I hope you have a good time, it ought to do you a lot of good.

I got your letter of the 21st last night Dad dear. Has the weather broken much or not. Out here it is very dull again now.

Yesterday evening half a dozen of us went into the neighbouring town to see the divisional concert there. It was a topping show and I had a jolly fine time. We caught a lorry coming back, when we clambered inside we found it was carrying 30.8 inch howitzer shells. We had some grand champagne cocktails just before the concert.

This morning I had to take C of E's to church and as no padre appeared we all beat it.

Well I am afraid there is nothing else to tell you now, so the best of luck to you all.

Your loving son,
Jack.

45. 27th May 1918 BEF, France.

My dear Mother and Father,

Our battalion concert party gave a topping a little show last night, there was quite a big crowd to see it. The show was in an old barn and two big farmyard gates had been lifted off their hinges and rested on ammunition boxes to make a stage. We got some sheets for a background, a clock, some pictures and furniture from knocked in houses and it made quite a bon stage. They got some old pots and put flowers in them and made footlights out of jam tins and candles. The girl in the party was dressed up in an old woman's clothes from a cottage.

Thanks very much for your letter Dad dear, I was pleased to get it and I am glad you are having a good time and feeling better, but have a good holiday this time not just one patch you up for a bit and then as soon as you get back to work again you will crock up.

Well I hope you are both very well.
Your loving son,
Jack.

P S.   Thanks for sending Gurgune's letter on to me Dad. Those pictures were of the Givenchy craters.

Enclosed is the identification disk of the German from whom I took the Iron Cross ribbon,

J.R. 362 = Jaeger Regiment 362. 22.3.91 is the date of his birth. Keitum Sylt is the name of the place where his home is. *(Sylt is an island in the North Sea just west of today's German/Danish border).*

46.   28th May 1918 BEF, France.

My dear Mother and Father,

I got your letter of 23rd last night Mother dear, it is good of you to write so often. I do enjoy getting letters from you both. I am afraid mine are a poor return for the trouble you both take. I don't want those pants, shirt & scarf back thanks and so far don't need any socks.

Wink is a lucky little beggar getting that chance of going to Devonshire for the summer hols, he ought to have a topping time. By the way how are his rabbits getting on and have they grown much.

Thanks for the letter Vera, you ask about Brigadier General Boyd Moss and if I know anything about him. He is in the same division and commands the ------- Brigade, the number of which is one less than my brigade. I am glad you are getting on well with your swimming.

Your letter of 23rd came also last night Dad dear. I don't know how you manage to keep on writing so much. I am sure I can't, but I do love getting them and I am glad you are getting better and having a good time.

That evening when I went into the burning town nearby it was a great sight. One whole street was blazing and there were clouds of thick black smoke going up. The place was full of gas that he had plunked into the place. One thing I knew I was safe going in, for as soon as his balloons see that smoke and flame, they leave off to gloat over it, really brother Fritz is an evil minded old swine.

The next day he set another village on fire just close by but it went out after a bit. He shells every village within reach now but our big guns are giving him a devil of a smashing. They shell him all night long with anything up to a 12 inch gun. Just imagine one of those shells exploding as it touches the road and throwing pieces about 1000 yards in every direction, that is what he is getting from us in this sector.

I wish you would send me out my other glengarry, a decent pair of light coloured khaki hosetops and a pair of khaki stockings, as I am rather in need of them.

A German steel helmet will start from here on its way shortly and with it a German groundsheet which Eric can keep for himself and use for camping. They are rather cute little things and can be rigged up as little tents. It ought to be just big enough for Eric.

Your loving son,
Jack.

P.S. This ground sheet was taken from a private of the 4th Guards reserve Division the last time I was up.
P.P.S. I had a grand bathe in a little stream yesterday afternoon. We had dammed it up with sandbags and made it deeper, so it is topping now. I had a tub before breakfast this morning also.

47. 28th May 1918 BEF, France.

My dear Mother and Father,

I got two more letters yesterday one from each of you. They were OK. I expect Eric is very excited about his trip to Devon.

Yesterday a French artillery officer came to tea with us in our hut. He was a good sport, we had a very good time, also he gave me his steel helmet as a souvenir. I am sending it back in a day or two with 1 or 2 other little things.

This afternoon we are having a boxing and wrestling show and I am running it. Of course that is if the weather permits.

We leave here this evening as the batt. comes out of rest and I go to it again for another rest.

I hope you are all fit and well.
Your loving son,
Jack.

48. 29th May 1918 BEF, France.

My dear Mother and Father,

I had a very good time yesterday evening. Eight of us walked over to a village about 6 kilos away to see our divisional party called 'The Roses' at the Army Mining School. Their show was a review called "How's this". It was a grand little show toppingly done, better than in an average provincial town, the fellows in it were nearly all pros.

There was a lightning sketch man in it, he did sketches of one or two fellows in the audience and caused great amusement. Then there was a topping conjurer there. One scene they had was in the trenches, it was awfully funny especially when a shell came across and plumped the other side of the trench. It was rather cutely done the whizz and bang. The best part was when a Boche came over to give himself up. The staging all through was topping, the dresses, make up, etc were bon, it is supposed to be one of the best shows in France.

On the way back we got a lift for part of the way in a lorry called an F.W.D. (four wheel drive) it means that all four wheels are driven instead of only the 2 back wheels and one of those lorries can move a 6 inch gun away at 10 mph.

Next time I go up to the line I think I shall try and get a good Boche greatcoat and send home and have it cleaned. It would make a good dressing gown don't you think. The German tin hat left here yesterday, I expect if the parcel gets away at all it will take about 8 days to get home. There is a shrapnel ball, French bullet and case (the big one), a German bullet and the very dirty looking cartridge case is the one I used to fire that 6 inch gun off with.

Do you think Vera could keep a record of all these things I send home; number them and keep a little book with all the information about them in it as the I expect if I go on sending all these things I shall soon forget all about them.

Well I hope you are all very well.
Your loving son,
Jack.

49. 30ᵗʰ May 1918 BEF, France.

My dear Mother and Father,

I got one letter from each of you last night both dated 25ᵗʰ, I was very pleased to get them. I think Wal Baker is jolly lucky getting home on leave. Yes the lily of the valley came from it.

The reason my letters get to you quickly now is because they leave in the afternoon, while when you are up in the line the letters cannot leave until dark. That means about 10 o'clock. A runner then goes off with them in a sandbag. They go back to company headquarters from there, where they are dumped in with the other platoons mail. Then they go back with a ration party to battalion headquarters.

From there they join the mail of the other companies and then put in limbers drawn by mules. They go back to the transport lines where the censors stamp is put on and they are sealed (the letters are actually censored up in the line by the platoon officer but the stamp is put on at the transport lines by the post corporal). Then they go back by lorries to the rail head and away home. So you can see the difference in time it takes for a letter to get to one from behind the line.

I expect to get into the line on 8th or 9th not the 5th as you say Mother dear. I wish you would let me know at what village he was hit and if it was at a place named Gorre, I think Uncle Pandy is lucky getting away with a decent wound like that.

I don't know why you both worry so much, it really is nothing like so bad as you think and except for an odd bit of bumping it is quite enjoyable in this grand weather. A kilt is A1 in this weather.

Well Dad I am very glad that parcel got home, I rather doubted it. You may find some of the things in it rather interesting especially their gas masks and pack. Now that I have the English, French and German masks, you will be able to see by comparison how much better ours are. What I want now is a French and Portuguese tin hat. They would look fine hanging up in the inner hall with that German one that I sent back.

I had a bathe yesterday afternoon in the stream and am going again today. I have been firing a Lewis gun (machine gun) this morning, hit a bottle at 100 yards with it. We had great sport.

Well I hope you are all going on well.
Your loving son,
Jack.

50. 31st May 1918 BEF, France.

My dear Mother and Father,

Had a busy morning today, left her at 10 on a reconnoitring job, got back here at 2. I went right up past Westminster Bridge, Vauxhall Bridge to Harley Street and then to a place where there has been a lot of heavy fighting in the earlier days of the war. Not Workman's Garden this time but to the right. Those names sound rather like towns, don't they. In this sector there are a lot of old pals. Finchley Road, Piccadilly Circus, Caledonian Road and tons of others. We could see the Boche line from where we stood, it was very quiet and a grand day. We saw 5 Boche planes up above us but they got it in the neck from our Archies and soon hooked it.

The country just behind the line looks wonderful. It is all marsh and covered with big trees and willows and reeds growing everywhere. Not very nice country to attack over and I think a good many fat Boche (if there are any now) would sink in the mud and peg out.

Well I am going to have a dip in the stream this afternoon, so goodbye for the present.

Your loving son,
Jack.

51. 1ˢᵗ June 1918 BEF, France.

My dear Mother and Father,

We have got a grand little fox terrier pup here now he sleeps under my bed in a box of straw, he is a topping little beggar to play with I wish I could send him home. Also I found a new pair of rubber thigh boots I shall hang on to them they would do fine for salmon fishing and wading.

This morning I had a bathe in the stream. I ran down before breakfast in my pyjamas, it was just topping. I went for a short walk this morning around the village. It is just on deserted except for a few troops in old cellars. The Boche has put gas and all sorts of shells into the place but we live just out of the way on the far edge of the village. The little church is quite alright inside but the town has had a few direct hits on it.

Well we leave here this afternoon for our old rest camp as the rest of the battalion comes out of the line tonight or early tomorrow morning.

Everything is going on very well out here. Nothing really unexpected has happened and it will be our turn in a month or two so don't worry about the old Boche's doings. I am very fit and well, the weather is absolutely grand.

I hope you are all having a very good time at home,

Your loving son,
Jack.

52. 2ⁿᵈ June 1918 BEF, France.

My dear Mother and Father,

What do you think of Maud Allan v. PB isn't it priceless. That is the only thing that seems to interest us out here. Nobody thinks of the scrapping that is going on north and down south.

(Maud Allan was a pianist turned actress, dancer and Choreographer once compared to Isadora Duncan. In 1918 the MP, Noel Pemberton in his own Journal 'Vigilante' published an article "The cult of the clitoris" which implied that Allen, appearing in 'The Vision of Salome' was a lesbian associate of German wartime conspirators. She sued him for libel which lead to a sensational court case which she lost).

Well my poor old captain, his runner and a stretcher bearer have all been killed in the last go up the line, awfully rotten. They got a 5.9 shell all to themselves. It was just chance.

Our new captain, who has just come from Ireland after a rest, is a wonderful fellow. He doesn't care a damn for anybody and is a fine hefty fellow. He has the Military Cross and Mons Star. He ticks the brigadier off in just the same as if he were a subaltern and all in such a slow deliberate way. One day the brig came round the line with Captain Davidson and saw some corrugated iron on the top of the trench to make a shelter for the boys. The brig asked why it was there so our old captain said, "Oh so that the rats can run across the top sir". The brig was quite annoyed.

Well I am very fit and well and am quite ready to get back in the line again, as you can do what you like up there and usually manage to have a good time. I have got 6 days left before I go up at least that or more not less. We moved successfully and are now in our new quarters with the rest of the batt.

I hope you have gone away Mother dear to get better yourself and to look after old Dad.

We are having wonderful weather here. I am very brown and fit. Has my parcel arrived yet?

Your loving son,
Jack.

53. 3rd June 1918 BEF, France.

My dear Mother and Father,

I received two letters from you yesterday Mother, one was in the parcel of chocolate, for which I thank you both very much, but it really isn't necessary as when we go up in the line we take one of those big wooden boxes of Frys chocolate with us

I was orderly officer today so had a little to do. I was superintending the bathing of our fellows from 8 to 11, seeing kilts were all fumigated properly. This afternoon the whole battalion is going to see the divisional show at the

Army Mining School. I am taking about 80 men of my company down at 5.

I am afraid that is not much else to say to you, so goodbye for the present. I am sorry you did not go away after all Mother dear. I don't think it is playing the game, as you must need it. I expect the garden looks fine now.

I do wish you wouldn't worry so much. What is the sense, I thought after a bit you would take things as a matter of course and not fidget. It does seem so silly.

Well the best of luck to you all.
Your loving,
Jack.

54.   6th June 1918 BEF, France.

My dear Mother and Father,

Everything is going well, and there is nothing much to say. The whole brigade had a lecture today on 'The spirit of the bayonet' by Colonel Campbell and the rest of the day was carried on in training.

No mail from home lately. I hope you are all very well. We are having great weather.

Your loving son,
Jack.

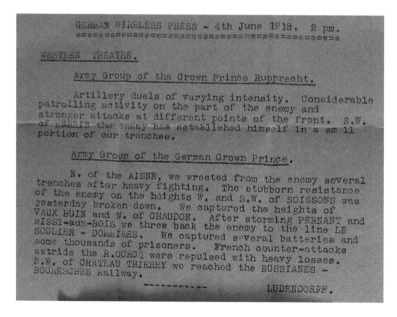

German Wireless Press, 4th June 1918

55.   7th June 1918   BEF, France.

My dear Mother and Father,

I got 6 letters yesterday, four from home (2 each) and two from Bedford. Also a parcel with the hosetops and stockings and chocolate. I am wearing shoes and stockings this afternoon, as it is hot and they are fine.

Well you seem to have had a good time Dad dear. I am glad of that. We had a pretty stiff little go this morning from 8 to 1 but in the afternoon there was a topping show in the wood. The brigade got it up, there was some show boxing and wrestling, the latter was jolly good. The massed bands played. Also our pipe band and there was highland dancing, one or two comic turns and one or two songs. It was an awfully enjoyable show. Today we only had a few parades and a show in the afternoon.

I am very glad parcel arrived with hat in it. No please don't try to polish it, it will spoil it altogether. That is the proper colour, so that it does not show up.

Your loving son,
Jack

56.   9th June 1918 BEF, France.

My dear Mother and Father,

I am glad you look so well again Dad dear. I think the 'calling up' must be a mistake, at any rate I hope so, as this is not the place for old men. That Webley I sent back was a spare one that a fellow gave me and not my own.

The weather has changed just a bit today. It looks rather like rain. We are having a very good time. There was a concert yesterday afternoon in the wood. It was quite a good show.

I wonder who sent me that parcel from Buzzards do you know?

Well goodbye for the present.
Your loving son,
Jack

57.   19th June 1918 BEF, France.

My dear Mother and Father,

We are having quite a good time here and it is very quiet. We came up 2 days ago or thereabouts.

I don't quite understand what you mean by 'that awful line'. I shall get fed up if you keep on worrying about me. You seem to think I am going through hell or some such place. Well it is all rot, there is nothing the matter with the place, we are having quite a good time. If you go on worrying at the rate you are at present going, I think you will break down, it seems to me to be so absurd. What have got to worry about I don't know.

We are in quite a pretty bit of country in a way at present. There is marshland all round us, with tons of willow trees and bushes all round and there are even rushes growing on the breastwork.

I saw four of our planes fooling about on top of his line this morning, he put quite a lot of shells and machine gun bullets at them. At about 4 this morning we saw quite a good little show of Very Lights put up by the Boche. He sent up orange, green, red and golden rain, ones that wiggle up like big snakes and all sorts.

Yesterday afternoon a lot of little balloons crossed our line on the way to the Boche. They are sent up by the Propaganda Department and carry pamphlets etc for him to read. They were all pale blue and white stripes. We potted at one as we wanted to see what it had got on board but we did not bring it down.

I had a letter from Bill Waldecker last night (*an American rowing friend from Bedford School*). They have not called him up yet. The enclosed reached me up in the line from Bill and I think you may find it interesting
.

There is not much else about him but he says if there are any stamps you want, will you let him know (*Jack's Father made a very valuable stamp collection*) his address is c/o Mrs M Cornell, 209 West 106th Street, New York. Syd is in the Columbia University 2nd VIII and is rowing 4.

Hope everything is A1 and please take to heart what I say.
You're loving son,
Jack.

58. 11th June 1918 BEF, France.

My dear Mother and Father,

We are having a top hole time, no shelling & grand weather. We shall be back in Reserve for a bit soon and I expect that will mean bathing in a canal.

Yesterday afternoon 2 of us put on gum boots and went up to the front line through the marshes. We had a look at his line and then came back. There are

3 of us who do trench patrol night & day. We do 2 hours on & 4 off for 4 days, it is quite a bon job.

Everybody is very cheery out here and things are going top hole. Have no more souvenirs yet but hope to get some soon. Some of those I sent back are interesting aren't they Dad. Has Uncle George or Uncle Billy seen them yet.

Well I hope you are all well at home.

Your loving son,
Jack.

59. 12ᵗʰ June 1918 BEF, France.

My dear Mother and Father,

We have moved from where we were before and are now right back for a few days. We are living in a breastwork that runs through a wood and the wood is in a marsh. It is very nice here and quite peaceful. The only things that bother us are the mosquitoes and of course the inevitable. Am going to have a bathe in the canal tomorrow.

Thanks very much for your letter of the 8ᵗʰ Dad dear, also Eric's epistle. The hose tops and stockings are A1 Mother dear. I'm glad Vera does so well in the swimming.

I think I shall send another German helmet home in a few days. I'll see what other things I get to send back first. By the way did that little bayonet arrive with the German pack and I wonder if you looked inside that German pack. You don't seem to like these souvenirs.

Enclosed are 2 pamphlets sent over by us in balloons to the Boche lines but these 2 blew back into our line and I found the picture in a shell hole that was full of water that's why it is so dirty. Don't you think it is awful trash, the Germans must think we are damn fools. Just look at the way it is drawn.

Best of luck,
Jack.

60. 14ᵗʰ June 1918 BEF, France.

My dear Mother and Father,

Am having a bon time here except for working parties every night.

Nothing doing today, did a little fish bombing today but not much luck. Also fired Very Lights into the water, they go in and keep alight down on the bottom and are great as fish killers. I tell you when we come home again fishing won't be such a slow past time as at present.

Everything is A1. Hope you are all well and cheery at home. I saw another crowd make a successful raid last night. It was a bon sight. They only had one slightly wounded. Old Fritz gave us a fine show of lights.

Hope you are all well.
Your loving son,
Jack.

61. 15th June 1918 BEF, France.

My dear Mother and Father,

I have done nothing interesting to tell you a present I am afraid but last night and the night before I was on a working party digging trenches. We leave here at 9:30 p.m. and arrive back at 3:30 am. They are a pretty fair sweat. We had a little of his sneezing gas this morning. You feel just as though you have got a very runny cold.

A Boche plane was over here this morning, he was very low down and got fired at like hell but got away. You could see the black crosses on his wings very plainly.

I don't know if you remember Darrock, a young tall fellow that came out with me. He had a near shave this morning. He was carrying a lot of cordite (explosive) in his apron pocket. Somehow or other it fired, burnt his kilt and legs badly and singed his eyelashes right off. He jumped into a stream to put himself out and will have to go to hospital. So that leaves only the company commander & 2 of us up here now.

Hope you are all well.
Your loving son,
Jack.

62. 16th June 1918 BEF, France.

My dear Mother and Father,

Now in the front line again and am afraid there are no things worth getting up here. I was out on patrol last night with four battalion scouts. We got through his wire and I heard one of them start coughing in a shell hole post. Then we heard some digging going on. And on the road behind I heard a Boche shout out.

Out in No Man's Land I found a pamphlet meant for the Boche. It is all about the Prime Minister's speech of 5th January 1918 I think. If you look through it you will see Ramsay MacDonald, Lord Lansdown, etc named in it. Yesterday when coming up here I saw one of our aeroplanes dropping pamphlets.

This morning the old Boche whizz banged us but you can stand right up against one without being touched, so they don't worry us much, the noise is the only thing about them.

Your loving son,
Jack.
PS. How are the rabbits going.

63.   18th June 1918 BEF, France.

My dear Mother and Father,

Everything going on well, we are at present having a fairly quiet time.

One funny thing about this place is the way the sparrows and birds seem to live up here. At present they are all chirping away in what remains of the trees, for we are in an old orchard at present.

By the time this letter reaches you I shall be back in rest.

Hope you are all well.

Your loving son,
Jack.

64.   21st June 1918. BEF, France.

My dear Mother and Father,

Am out of the line now and am quite fit.
Will write soon,
Jack.

65.   23rd June 1918 BEF, France.

My dear Mother and Father,

I expect you will wonder why I have not written a letter for such a long while but it has been impossible as I had a very busy time up the line for the last four days and back here we have not had a minute to ourselves until today (Sunday) and now I only got off parade at 4 o'clock.

Well there is nothing to write about really. We have been busy reorganising after our trip and cleaning up kit, Lewis guns etc.

I saw one of our balloons brought down in flames yesterday.

I am still quite fit but a devil of a lot of officers and men are down with P.U.O. *(Pyrexia (fever) of Unknown Origin).*

Hope you are all well at home. What a pity the garden boy is going. You asked about sending parcel out. I would rather like a few sugar sweets occasionally.

Your loving son,
Jack.

66. 24th June 1918 BEF, France.

My dear Mother and Father,

Things are still going on well. I got a letter from you this afternoon Mother dear. You all seem to be having quite a good time at home.

Well there is nothing to tell you. I have been a bit unwell during the morning and afternoon but am now fit again. A very big number are going sick here and the Boche is worse off still.

Well goodbye.
Your loving son,
Jack.

67. 25th June 1918   BEF, France.

My dear Mother and Father,

The weather has broken a good deal here and it is now cloudy and rainy. I was unable to get any souvenirs up the line this time but hope to next trip.

The place where I was in reeked of dead but that is all. It was so bad and the flies so thick that even the troops eat very little and I had a lot of sick from the place.

Kellie the officer who was in the south keep was killed by a Minnie. I was in the North keep.

Enclosed is a cheque for you Dad dear for your birthday and will you get me £50 of War Savings Certificates with the other cheque.

Enclosed is a book on the division. I was in the scrapping from the 11th. I am afraid it is not very interesting but still.

Hope you are all well.
Your loving son,
Jack.

68. 28th June 1918 BEF, 15 Platoon, 1st Liverpool Scottish.

My dear Mother and Father,

We came up the line last night and I am now in a very comfortable little spot by the canal. The weather has turned fine and hot again and I am going to have a bathe later on.

I got your letter of 23rd yesterday Mother dear. I am sorry Eric is queer.

I expect the garden is topping now, you ought to take a photo with my little camera, then I could see what it is like. I expect Eric has got something the same as is affecting a lot of fellows out here.

I was in charge of a party of 30 carrying duckboards up to the front line. It took us from 9:30 to 12:30. And then you always stand-to from 3 to 4 each morning. Then a bit more sleep.

I had a topping swim this afternoon. The canal is grand and warm. 6 men of my platoon were in also, so it was quite good sport. It didn't seem possible that only a mile away is front line.

I am living in a fine little shack, I have an old wire netting bed in there, but for meals we all mess together (3 of us) in an old house on the canal bank.

Thank you very much for your letter Dad dear. I saw in a paper out here that Eton won, but nothing else. The old school (*Bedford*) didn't do too badly.

Well I hope you are all very fit.
Your loving son,
Jack.

69. 29th June 1918 15th Ptn Z coy, 1st Liverpool Scottish, BEF, France.

My dear Mother and Father,

Thanks very much for letter of the 24th I am very glad Wink is better again, I hope he will pick up again quickly.

Poor old Auntie Tina I expect she was in an awful stew about moving. Has she sold you any part worn tins of butter etc. I suppose she has been trying to do some bargaining.

I hope you will be able to get another garden boy as Dad will only knock himself up again if you can't.

I had a bathe in the canal yesterday afternoon, I think I shall go in again today but it is a bit colder. Yesterday evening we had a heavy thunderstorm for a while, it has cleared things up a bit. I suppose it was badly needed but it makes things a lot harder out here as all the tracks and paths get very muddy and slippery and everything gets delayed. Then also it is more difficult to see your way as the path does not show up white when wet.

Quite a good little show up here a night or two ago. Shall be going in, south of Workman's Garden in a few nights time.

Am feeling very fit again now. Had a letter from Noah Robertson he is in the 17th Northumberland Fusiliers out here. He rowed bow in the house IV the last time I rowed (*He is in the photo of Crescent House IV shown later*).

Has Miss Sley translated any of those pamphlets yet, I daresay one of them would be rather interesting.

I hope you are all well at home.
Your loving son,
Jack.

PS. Have those two cheques arrived yet.

70.   30th June 1918 BEF, France.

My dear Mother and Father,

I got your letter of 25th last night Dad dear. What a funny idea thinking I have been hit or ill, there is nothing the matter with me and I am up in the line having quite a bon time.

Thanks very much for getting the Sporting and Dramatic News (*English weekly magazine founded in 1874 and became Sport and Country, then Farm and Country, before closing in 1970*) for me they will be A.1. for my album.

It is in a way a good job that Bateman's have left. Auntie was such an awful fidget wasn't she.

I had another ripping swim yesterday afternoon. There were about 10 of the men in also, it was quite bon.

Last night I was in charge of a carrying party of 33 men. We were out from 11:30 p.m. to 2 o'clock carrying duckboards up to the front line. "Rest and be thankful" and "Rest for the weary". The last two places are old houses that are fortified.

This morning I went along to the baths and had a hot bath in a big beer barrel cut in half. The water is pumped out of the canal into tin cans which are heated on a fire. Some way of bathing isn't it. Especially as it is within a mile of front line. The regiment that we relieved up here had a few casualties at those same baths when they were here.

We are having grand weather here it is boiling hot again, I'm going to have another swim this afternoon. Tonight we leave here and go up a little closer for the next four days. It is a very bon spot that we are going to, the only drawback is that we shall not be near the canal and bathing will be napoo.

I hope to get a Boche tin hat when we get into front line for the last 4 days or so.

We had a bit of revolver practice at bottles and tins in the canal yesterday afternoon. I am quite a dab at it now and could hit a wine bottle at 20 yards floating in the water pretty well every time. My revolver is exactly the same as that one you have at home.

Next time I am out I will send an English Chapeau de Feu back and will put a little letter inside asking you to take it to Dunns the Hatter to have a patent inside put in it. Don't send it but keep it, it is only in case the parcel is opened, as Government property is not to be sent home and I have a good excuse then for sending it if it gets opened. Tell me if this letter gets home alright.

It is damn fine out here in this weather only it seems such a waste of time.

How is Auntie Beatty and Uncle Dick getting on. Also Auntie and Uncle George and the boy, they must be having a topping time this weather. I expect the garden looks ripping now.

Well I will close now as I am just ready for lunch which consists of a chop, pork and beans and mashed potatoes, so we are evidently winning the war at present.

By the ways things are going toppingly out here and the Americans are jolly good fighters.

Best of luck to you all.
Your loving son,
Jack.

71. 1ˢᵗ July 1918 France.

My dear Mother and Father,

Am now in a different place again. It is very good and comfortable here and fairly quiet. We are busy on the trench and even after today's work it looks quite different.

I am at present in charge of the left half company and tonight I will be in charge of the company just until the following night.

The weather is A.1. and we miss the canal, it was rotten leaving the bathing place.

I hope you are all well at home.
Your loving son,
Jack.

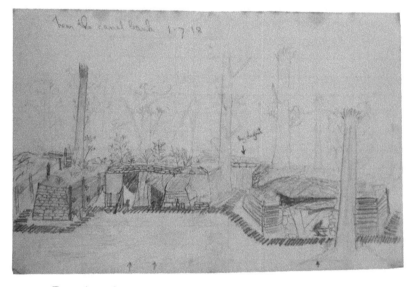

Drawing of trench near the canal bank. Letter 1ˢᵗ July 2018

72. 2ⁿᵈ July 1918 BEF, France.

My dear Mother and Father,

I am getting on in fine style now. We have been putting up some very hot defences and traps in our bit of trench and having a good time, it is good fun.

Poor old Tubby Myles got pinched two nights ago by some Boches while out on patrol. The battalion is out for blood.

Thanks very much for your letters (including Atchy's). We whacked 3 Boche the other night by getting out to one of his shell hole posts, which he only occupies at night. The fellows got out (500 yards from our line) and waited in this post for him to come out and occupy it. He came out and the three Boche went west but our fellows had to clear out as he started bombing them out. They were not my company.

Enclosed is the Post Office pamphlet which I have filled in.

No more news at present. I hope everything is going well at home.
Your loving son,
Jack

73. 5th July 1918 BEF, France.

My dear Mother and Father,

I am up in front line again for a spell, it is not such a bad little spot. I live in a house built up with reinforced concrete, that is during the day.

I have got a Boche tin hat up here and some ammunition pouches, but I don't know if they will get back to rest billets as I have a lot to carry out as it is, and it is a long march back.

Back in the line where I have just left we had great sport shooting at Boche planes whenever they came over our line. One of my guns fired 1,200 rounds one day and I then had 4 guns and we had them all going and the other fellows engaging the Boche with rifles, we used to raise a hell of a din. Some of their planes used to fire back at us with tracer bullets but they did not get near us. Last night there were twenty of our planes up above and over our lines. The old Boche was archeying away at them all the time.

Earlier on in the afternoon I saw three of our little fighters go diving down onto his line and open their machine guns on him when only 50 feet up. Then they would shoot up into the air again.

P.U.O stands for P---- of Unknown Origin (*Pyroxia*). I can't remember what the P stands for but any doctor would tell you. It is a sort of Flanders Fever.

Thanks very much for your letter of 26th Mother dear. I shall be lucky if I get leave in another 6 months.

Hope you are all very fit at home.

Don't worry,
Your loving son,
Jack.

74. 6th July 1918 BEF, France.

My dear Mother and Father,

I had an interesting little time last night out on patrol. We got 400 yards out and between two of his posts, did not see or find much. The grass was nearly up to your knees so crawling along you were very nearly hidden. We were out from 11:15 to 2:30. We came across a Boche track and found one of his duckboards over an old trench, a respirator, tin hat and a potato masher (stick-bomb). We thought we had got a Boche in an old trench as we saw this stick-bomb on the parapet and thought he had ducked down. You should have seen two of my fellows whip into the trench with their bayonets drawn, but no luck. I brought the stick-bomb in and have emptied the explosive out, also the detonator, so it is quite safe. You have to be careful of these bombs lying out in No Man's Land as there may be string tied to it and when you pick it up it goes off. There are all sorts of tricks like that.

Up here our planes are very active and the old Boche archeys away like hell at them.

I am very fit and well and am having quite a respectable time. I can even wash every morning and we have a fine little dugout in an old house that is reinforced with concrete. I live in here with my two sergeants, one with the Military Medal (Sergeant Bell) and the other the Distinguished Conduct Medal (Sergeant Macrae). The latter was amateur middleweight wrestler of the north of England. My servant lives in here and cooks the meals, keeps the place clean and gets water from shell holes for washing purposes.

I hope you are all fit and well.
Your loving son,
Jack.

75. 7th July 1918 BEF, France.

My dear Mother and Father,

Nothing to tell you this time, at present we are having a quiet time. Our planes are very active, 16 of them came over this evening.

I do hope things are well at home. Well by the time this reaches you I expect to be out in rest again.

The mosquitoes and flies bother us here a good deal especially knees and thighs, that is one drawback for a kilt. One of the fellows has made me a pair of breeches out of sand bags for patrolling, I keep my kilt on underneath just the same.

Well goodnight to you and may you sleep well. This is the busy time out here.

Your loving son,
Jack.

76. 8th July 1918 BEF, France.

My dear Mother and Father,

We had rather a lively little night yesterday. First the Boche started and then we did. We bumped hell out of him, at least some of his shell hole posts. Then our patrol crawled out, got in it and got what they could. The idea is to get a wounded or dead man or papers clothes etc belonging to them, so to find out what regiment you are up against. I got a leather belt with a brass buckle, on it was a crown with "Gott mit uns" on it (God with us). 2 great coats, a pack & a rifle were brought in. We found a shirt, pair of drawers and a few odds and ends in the pack including an English cigarette tin with soap in it. The regiment was 203rd Old Pals from the 9th April. By the way what numbers have I got now. I have sent a few haven't I.

This morning we took turns to have pot shots with the old Boche rifle. We fired 20 rounds altogether. This afternoon I was up a ladder behind our house having a look at his line. It is very interesting looking right behind his lines.

Enclosed are one or two Scarlet Pimpernels from No Man's Land. I got them this morning while the mist was very thick this morning.

The Old Man was very windy last night, he thought we were coming over this morning I think. He kept sending up orange lights during the night (these mean gas I think) as he was getting plenty from us. He also sent up cherry brandy and creme de menthe lights and this morning he was standing-to in his advanced posts and he kept firing into the mist. At times he sent 'pineapples' over. These are light minenwerfer. Their real name is granatenwerfer. We call the bigger minnies 'rum jars'.

Old Joe worried us a bit as he held the rations limbers up for a long time owing to bumping the roads. We thought we would have to do without grub for today and that would have brought the war home to us properly.

I got your parcel up early this morning it was very bon but as you have a job don't worry any more please. Rough luck about Critchley pipping it. I am sorry for Dorothy. By jove currants and cherries seem to be some price.

I hope you get right quickly Dad dear. By the time this gets home I shall be out on rest with luck.

Hope you are all very well.
Your loving son,
Jack.

Enclosed is a paper packet to put that German tobacco in that I sent home earlier. Also a shoulder strap and a great coat button. The bit of linen came off a pair of German PANTS.

77. 10ᵗʰ July 1918 BEF, France.

My dear Mother and Father,

I am now out of the front line and am in charge of a half company guarding a bridge on the canal bank. We live in big iron shacks built into the bank. It is not too warm today so I don't know if I shall bathe yet.

I saw quite a good little scrap yesterday morning. First a Boche plane dived out of the clouds and drove down one of our reconnaissance planes. Then one of our little scouts came up and attacked the Boche. They scrapped for a bit and circled round each other and then both beat it to their own lines.

I have got some souvenirs for home this time, at least they have come out of the front line with me:-
Boche tin hat, belt, ammunition pouches and potato masher (stick bomb).

I had a ripping swim this evening and feel quite grand again. You see I have not had my boots off for 6 days and that makes your feet a bit soft. I shall have done 16 days in the line before getting back in rest again. Only 3 days rest this time, then comes another dozen in the line.

We can see the Boche line from here, that is if you get up on top of the bank. Funnily enough we are guarding an old pal named Westminster Bridge.

Couldn't send you a letter yesterday as there is no mail on the night you come out of the line. Hope everything is A1 at home. I am feeling very fit. I slept from 7 this morning till 4 in the afternoon and am going to sleep nearly all tonight just to put myself right again. No lying out in No Man's Land while we are here.

Your loving son,
Jack.

78. 11ᵗʰ **July 1918 BEF, France.**

My dear Mother and Father,

I had quite a good view of a raid by us last night. At least I could see the shells bursting and also a wonderful display of coloured lights by old Joe, double orange lights, double reds and greens. He also sent up a wonderful rocket that burst into golden, red, orange and green lights. It's a great sight. You could see his Minnies going up and come shooting down with a devil of a crash. They have big red tails of sparks and give you a devil of a shaking up if you are anywhere near.

We are having a ripping time down here. My fellows are all grand and comfortable and so am I. In fact I don't want to go out on rest. We all had a ripping swim this afternoon and we are only 900 yards away from the front line.

I am doing fine at present and am enjoying myself very much.

I hope you are all very well.
Your loving son,
Jack.

79. 13ᵗʰ **July 1918 BEF, France.**

My dear Mother and Father,

I arrived out of the line early this morning. We had 16 days this trip. I had my usual swim in the canal yesterday afternoon it was a bit colder but very nice when once you were in the water.

We came out in great style, the troops were singing hard all the way back. When I got back to my shack I found a letter from each of you waiting for me. I was very glad to get them, you seem to be having a good time at home.

I had a good sleep this morning, got up at 10 and had breakfast, then took a bathing parade at 11. Am just off on parade, so goodbye till tomorrow.

Your loving son,
Jack.

80.   15th July 1918 BEF, France.

My dear Mother and Father,

Am going up the line tonight. Will send a longer letter to you tomorrow as I am very busy at present.

Hope everything is A1. Got a parcel from Auntie Mabel yesterday.

Your loving son,
Jack.

81.   16th July 1918 BEF, France.

My dear Mother and Father,

I am in a fairly good little spot, only water half up your legs whenever you move. My position is in some little bits of posts out in a marsh, very pleasant, full of mosquitoes and frogs. One of my fellows got bitten by a rat in the ear and had to go down to have it dressed. The water about the place is rotten. We have had terrific rain storms lately and the canal has broken its banks in this part (at least the Boche did it).

I am very fit and well and the weather was very hot today, like a Turkish bath in the marsh. I am enjoying myself pretty well paddling in the water. One track I went along at 2 this morning, water was up to my knees but a kilt is very useful as it floats out in the water if you fall in a shell hole.

I sent a parcel off yesterday. Will give you particulars tomorrow. The handkerchief case is for you.

Your loving son,
Jack.

82.   17th July 1918 BEF, France.

My dear Mother and Father,

Things are going fine all round out here. Also I am being relieved and going down on a short rest tonight. Darroch is taking my place, he has just been away on a gas course.

The weather is very hot still and today I am going to try to get away and have a swim in the canal. I was out last night in charge of a big working party, it was very hot like being in a Turkish bath.

The parcel sent home contains a Boche tin hat, Boche equipment belt pouches and cap, French cap and English lachrymatory (tear gas goggles). Also a handkerchief case with the divisional rose on it for you, Mother dear.

I think I put a photo of my batman in but am not sure. He is a great lad, an Irishman and as broad a brogue as possible and as cute as they make them.

I hope everything is going OK at home.
Your loving son,
Jack.

83.   19th July 1918 BEF, France.

My dear Mother and Father,

I got a letter dated 12th from you today, Mother dear. Will you give me Julie's address please so that I can write and thank her.

I am living in a ripping wood now and having quite a good time. Today I borrowed a bicycle to ride up to brigade headquarters (about 8 miles away) to represent my battalion in a conference about boxing competitions in the brigade.

The fowls have done jolly well, the old ones don't seem to be getting tired out do they?

There is nothing much else to say for the present but I got a long letter from Syd (*Waldecker*) the other day. He is getting on fine and Bill (*his brother*) is in the American Flying Corps.

I hope you are all very well at home.
Your loving son,
Jack.

84.   20th July 1918 BEF, France.

My dear Mother and Father,

We had a great do last night as one of our fellows is going as second in command to a regiment in another division. We had a real blind on mixed Vermouth etc. Had the pipers playing outside and then a couple of them absolutely blind marching round the mess playing. We had Highland flings & ragging. One fellow that had gone to bed was raided, hauled into the mess in his pyjamas and court marshalled by the junior subs. The mess waiters were blind and it was a wonderful night.

The weather is tophole and so is the country round here. You would not know there was a war on. Only at night Boche planes come over pretty often.

I am having a ripping rest here. Has that volume of the Ousel *(Bedford School magazine)* come back from Hockliffes, the bookbinders of Bedford, yet please *(He had them all leather bound to keep for posterity)*.

Hope everything is A1.
Your loving son,
Jack.

85. 21ˢᵗ July 1918 BEF, France.

My dear Mother and Father,

Am having a bon time. I stayed off parade all the morning and went on a tactical scheme in the afternoon and went for a stroll over to the transport lines in the evening.

Nothing else to say at present. A ripping parcel came from Mrs Christy yesterday.
Your loving son,
Jack.

86. 22ⁿᵈ July 1918 15th Ptn Z coy, 1ˢᵗ Liverpool Scottish, BEF, France.

My dear Mother and Father,

Two of us went out to tea with a French artillery officer yesterday afternoon. We had quite a good time, they live in a railway train, travel in it and all, in fact they have a very bon time. With a little bit of luck I am going to get a tin hat out of him in a day or two.

The news is pretty good isn't it.

Enclosed is a pamphlet from Ireland and a label of one of our divisional soda water bottles. Some swank eh?

Last night we had another little feed. I am afraid you will be wondering what is coming over me but life out of the line is rather slow so it has to be livened up.

I hope the garden etc is going well and likewise all of you at home. Has my parcel arrived yet and has that volume of the Ousel come back yet.

Your loving son,
Jack.

87. 24th July 1918 BEF, France.

My dear Mother and Father,

I did not write yesterday as there was absolutely nothing to tell you yesterday and today is the same. I just went for a little walk in the evening around the country. It is very pretty about here, well wooded and hilly. We have had very heavy rainstorms lately that it has not been advisable to move very far away from here so I have only been around the camp.

I bought a pair of field boots yesterday from another fellow for 20 francs. They are pretty well brand new. I have also a pair of rubber thigh boots and two pairs of ankle boots so I am pretty well off for boots.

I received a letter from Dorothy yesterday which I will acknowledge now. Things are going A1 out here.

I hope you are all very fit and well and of the garden is going A1.

Your loving son, Jack.

88. 27th July 1918 BEF, France.

My dear Mother and Father,

I got 3 letters yesterday, one from you Mother of 18th & 21st and one from you Dad of 20th. I was very glad to get them and they were fine and long. I hope you had a bon birthday Dad dear. I shouldn't have minded being home for that. Those were two ripping letters you sent me Mother dear and at last you seem to have cheered up. I can assure you I am having a bon war out here.

I am very glad the parcel arrived safely as the tin hat is a good specimen also the belt. Did you notice the motto on it of "God is with us."

Thanks very much Dad dear for your letters. I am glad the bazaar was such a success. Am very busy over some boxing and wrestling competition.

So goodbye for the present, Jack.

89. 29th July 1918 BEF, France.

My dear Mother and Father,

Yesterday afternoon the rain kept off and we had quite a good little boxing and wrestling show, it lasted for two hours and there was some really good scrapping.

I have now left the old camp and am up with the battalion in rest. We are in a ripping little camp now in iron huts and as the weather seems to have altered now, they are sweltering hot.

I don't know if I told you that I bought a decent pair of field boots for 20 francs from another fellow, they are A.1.

I shall be sending that French tin hat in a day or two but I'm afraid it may get damaged on the way home as they are rather fragile.

Now for some interesting news. Last time up in the line one of our officers went out with 3 men in daylight to the Boche line. They were all in patrol suits made of green waterproof canvas and grass plated around their necks and blacked faces with grass stuck in their hair and reeds covering their faces.

They got through the Boche wire (3 belts of it) and spotted a sentry in his line. They dodged him and got into a post where they went through the men's kit, took 2 rifles and 1 or 2 caps, as there were no men in the post. Then round came a big Boche with a black beard. The officer had a shot at him and missed. The Boche promptly unslung his rifle and shot, missed. Then Rathbone had his second shot and did the trick. They then cleared out and had to dodge from shell hole to shell hole as a machine gun from another post opened on them every time they appeared. The four of them got home alright, one slightly wounded in the backside by a spent bullet. They had about 400 yards to go, 150 of which were in full view of the enemy, then the bushes, hedges and long grass hid them from view. They got in alright.

Another patrol crawled down a ditch in a devil of a thunderstorm, got into a post, captured 3 Boche and a machine gun and took them back in.

Your loving son,
Jack.

90. 31ˢᵗ July 1918

I am very fit and the parcel was absolutely ripping, especially the cakes. The sweets are the best I have had so far.

My battalion has been chosen to represent the company in a battalion wiring competition, so I am very busy with that and the boxing. Will write a long letter when I get the time.

Your loving son,
Jack.

91. 4th August 1918 BEF, France.

My dear Mother and Father,

The boxing went off in great style yesterday morning, there was some real good fighting.

The day before I was in charge of my company in a brigade route march and tactical scheme. I had to ride a horse & did alright at trotting and cantering, at any rate we did a good few miles and I did not come off. It poured with rain all the time, but I thoroughly enjoyed.

I am now up the line in charge of this company, we are having a good time. You know the famous hall at home where German officers live, well that is where I am living, only out here.

The weather has changed now and is ripping. This morning I saw an air fight, our plane went for Boche and chased him away from our line. It was quite a good scrap. A parcel has left for home, the cross is made of French bullets.

Mrs Higgs brother, who is a corporal in Y company is coming home for a commission, ask Mrs Higgs about him (*Jack transferred from Z to Y company sometime after this*). I told him to come over and see you as he lives opposite. He is an awfully good fellow, you will like him very much and he will tell you a lot.

I hope you are all very well at home and that everything is OK.

Your loving son,
Jack.

P.S. In enclosed photo Darroch is in the back row. Note Yankee officer sitting on right. Darroch was on a course at the time.

92. 5th August 1918 BEF, France.

My dear Mother and Father,

Just a line to let you know I am alive and kicking. My company was mentioned today by the brigadier for having the cleanest trenches in the brigade sector and my platoon for having the best kept post in the line.

Today we brought a Boche plane down with Lewis gun fire. It came down in the Boche line. The cheeky beggar flew up and down my front, so all guns and rifles opened on him and he is now napoo.

I hope everything is going well.
Jack.

93.   8th August 1918 BEF, France.

My dear Mother and Father,

I expect you are wondering why you have not heard from me lately, but I have been rather busy & not had time to write. We are now back in the old wood again and having a peaceful time. I am still in command of my company in place of the skipper who is having a rest.

Old Rathbone got another Boche yesterday, crept out with a daylight patrol, found a sentry and put a bullet through his head. Another patrol got out into a Boche keep, found a light machine gun with no sentry near it, found the team of 4 men asleep in a dugout, woke them up, shot one who tried to shoot, made the other three carry the M.G. back to our line.

Another Patrol went out, got in his line when 40 Boche came out into No Man's Land to cut them off. One of our flanking Lewis guns got on to them and napooed them. I won't tell you anymore but these doings are occurring daily. There is good news up here. I expect you will read about it soon.

Am going to have a bathe in the canal this afternoon I think if the weather keeps fine.

Your loving son,
Jack.

94.   13th August 1918 BEF, France.

My dear Mother and Father,

I have had quite an interesting day today. The weather has been great and so has observation. I watched a Boche post through a telescope, could see the sentry in one of those little round caps looking all over the place. I saw an officer in a black peaked cap go up the trench and speak to the sentry. I saw another sentry later on in the same place. It was very interesting watching these sentries, I could see them scanning the ground with glasses, they were very much on the alert.

I saw a Boche anti-aircraft gun firing at one of our planes and had a look at one of his sausages (*Balloons*). It had a big black cross painted on its side.

I hope you are getting better. I am very glad you say it is getting on well, Mother dear. I sent a Whizzbang (postcard) off to Eric yesterday.

Has that French tin hat come yet. I hope it turns up safely as it is rather a good little one.

I am feeling very fit and so far we are having a really bon time.
Your loving son,
Jack.

P.S. How is the rowing going, Dad dear.

95.   14th August 1918 BEF, France.

My dear Mother and Father,

Everything is going well. I am having quite a good time up in the front line. The weather is awfully hot and the nights are drawing out now.

The country around here is very green, it is all overgrown and little willows everywhere. The houses are just piles of brick and in places there is an odd cellar in which you can live. The belts of wire in No Man's Land are half covered over by long grass and weeds and there are bushes and dry ditches everywhere.

I got your letter of the 9th last night Mother dear, I am glad that French hat got back alright, what do you think of it, old Dad will have a collection to wear on air raid nights now. That cross was made out of French bullets. Last night I collected a German gas mask made of leather instead of rubber, I will send it back soon.

I shall be out of the line by the time this reaches you and away on a musketry course for about a fortnight, so you will be able to easy down for a bit.

I hope you will get right quickly Mother dear and that you are both fit and well.
Jack.

96.   17th August 1918 1st Liverpool Scottish, 1st Corps School, Musketry BEF.

My dear Mother and Father,

We came out of the line yesterday and this morning I started for this place and arrived this evening, it is about a 12 days course and I am fed up to the neck with it already. It is right away from the war. We are in a hut just by a little village, a sweet little place and the country is great but awfully dull. I shall not know what to do with myself. Of course I just miss the brigade boxing by coming on this damn course, also the divisional horse show.

I had a ripping time up the line this time, I really enjoyed myself, I really mean this. It was very interesting watching Boche behind his line. We also had some good sport with brother Boche in the way of sniping. One morning 4 of them were standing on the parapet, the mist suddenly lifted and disclosed them. They got a Lewis gun pan emptied into them and went down with a bang. We also had a Boche rifle that one of my fellows found in a post. We cleaned it up and used it on him.

Rather a funny thing happened one night. Movement was reported in front and two fellows went along a hedge to spot, (they both left from different posts) they met each other and both thought each other Boche. They both dropped their riles and went for each other, one had a couple of teeth knocked out and the other was laid out by the other putting a kick to his privates, the fellow fairly yelled and nearly got bayoneted by a party of our fellows that came up.

Well I hope you are all well,
Jack.

97.   18th August 1918   1st Corps School, Musketry, BEF.

My dear Mother and Father,

I had a ripping day today. I went out for a good walk this morning also afternoon. We found one or two nice little country pubs.

The country around here is ripping but walking is the only thing to do.

I hope everything is going well at home and that you are all fit.
Your loving son,
Jack.

98.   21st August 1918   1st Corps School, Musketry.

My dear Mother and Father,

I am very busy here, so please excuse short scrawl. Commission Paper enclosed is quite correct. It means I do an odd parade or two for 4 years from time of gazette (just as before war).

I am fit and well but will be glad to get back to my batt. although I'm having a very good time here and they are a good lot of fellows. I had a bon bath today. The weather is very hot out here but the country is grand. It is impossible to realise there is a war on.

Those two letters I got (one from each) were very nice I am glad you are feeling so well Dad dear and the rowing is going so strong, it must do you a lot of good, you <u>must</u> keep it up, but can't you take things a bit easier you'll only do yourself in again.

I suppose the post girl does know my parcels by now, they are certainly a fairly useful size in those old sandbags. I suppose the people at home find them a bit interesting.

By the way have you found out if that Corporal Chambers (Mrs Higgs brother) is home yet, you must get hold of him, he is an awfully nice fellow, an old Barts man and mighty interesting.

Well olly olly,
Chip chip,
Jack.

P.S. I got a letter from Vera yesterday.

99. 25th August 1918   1st Corps School.

My dear Mother and Father,

We have been having some fun nights recently after much hard work. There are three of us here from the Scottish, the other 2 are both huge fellows and after dinner we raise merry hell every night in the ante room, dancing, singing, scrumming and having a real rag. At first the other fellows (about 100 of them) were slow but we woke them up (you see it is a tradition that the Scottish always takes the lead).

Well last night was a wonderful show, some dopey fellows began playing bridge instead of joining in the ragging, so we had a pukka charge and cleared the mess. Everything was overturned and the whisky buzzed around, it was great sport. Then we had rugger scrums and tackling etc. It was like a real old Scottish guest night at home.

When we finally went to bed another mob tried to raid us but we soused them with buckets of water that we had kept handy in our hut (we are not green). We then followed up with a charge and completely routed the crowd. It's a great relaxation after the line and great sport.

Yesterday afternoon I had a very enjoyable time went into _____ in a lorry, 11 kilos away (5 miles = 8 kilos) it was a topping run through ripping country. I had a damn nice tea there and bought a few collars and ties and a shirt. There were quite a few Yanks knocking about there.

I have received quite a bunch of letters from you both since I have been here and I'm awfully glad everything is going so well. You must be getting quite fit now Dad dear, I expect the rowing is doing it. Perhaps it is a good job in a way Mother dear that you cannot get about much as you must be having a much needed rest and it ought to do you good especially with the ripping weather.

The old man is getting a thin time now. I feel an awful slacker down here and am fed up with being kept down here, although I am having a bon time.

I sent the War Bond paper off long ago.

I hope you are all A1 at home.
Your loving son,
Jack.

100. 27th August 1918   1st Corps School. France.

My dear Mother and Father,

I received your parcel 2 days ago the cakes were A.1. but the box was badly battered and really would not be serviceable again.

I have been to a couple of concerts here given by the "Very Lights", not bad shows really.

I am sorry your leg is still so rotten Mother dear. I do wish it would get better quickly.

Well what do you think of our little push, jolly good work. All along the line our fellows seem to be doing jolly well. He'll be back in the Hindenburg Line again soon and don't be surprised if he is not out of France this year.

Well I hope you are all very cheery at home. Have you seen Mrs Higgs yet about her brother. You will find he will be able to tell you a devil of a lot.

I hope you are all very fit.
Your loving son,
Jack

101. 29th August 1918   1st Corps School.

My dear Mother and Father,

I am getting on fine here, have won quite a bit of money from the shooting on the miniature range. Yesterday we went to the big range, up to 500 yard range where it poured with rain all day we got pretty wet and had to beat it.

Well I hope Vera got back alright and had a good time & that you are still keeping the weight up Dad dear. Is your leg better Mother dear.

Your loving son,
Jack.

102. 3rd September 1918 1st Corps School.

My dear Mother and Father,

I go back to my batt on the 4th and I am very glad although I have had a good time here. I suppose you have seen in the papers about our push at G-------.

(Givenchy? This had been held against the German Spring Offensive of 9th April, 1918. The 55th Division held their ground against this major assault, despite the Portuguese being overwhelmed (referred to in an earlier letter as The Porker Cheese), *and so thwarted the German aim of reaching the Channel Ports and the disaster of cutting British supply lines. It was in this offensive that Uncle Pandy was wounded. He was was in the same Division as Jack.*

Jack arrived in France on 3rd April, just before this Offensive, so was lucky not to be in the thick of this battle).

I laugh when I read your letter about that picture of a Boche I would like to see your face when you opened it. You may expect me home on leave in ------ December, not before.

Have you seen Mrs Higgs about her brother yet? I am afraid these notes are very short and far between but when I get back to the old batt I will write more but I am very busy at nights here. I got a very good report here and was recommended to be an instructor.

Enclosed is a letter from a corporal who was in my platoon, about the souvenir hunting. I had a near shave with him about 3 months back when I got that Boche and his iron cross ribbon in daylight early one misty morning. Nearly all these souvenirs you've got I got in No Man's Land but I am very careful now.

I am glad the Wink had such a bon holiday. When are you going Mother dear. Perhaps now Dad will drop working so hard as Uncle Dick is back.

I hope you are all going very strong and fit and well.
Your loving son,
Jack.

P.S. What do you think of the war, our TAILS ARE VERY MUCH UP, you watch things closely. I wonder when the 'Red Rose Jocks' (*reference to the 55th (West Lancashire) Division Liverpool Scottish*) are going over again, don't worry yet, but he'll be on the run soon, and then YANKS.

Transcribed letter: |
No. 16 Officer Cadet Battalion Club,
Bodelwyddan House,
Rhuddlan,
North Wales.

Cadet W. Chadwick,
No 16 O.C.B.
"C" Coy. Hut 36,
Kummell Park,
Rhyl.

Dear Mr Beresford,

I thought perhaps you would like to know what part of the world I had been sent to since taking my leave of the platoon.

I got my usual 2 weeks leave on arrival in England but managed to wangle another week. Had to report to No.1 Reception Battalion., Ripon, a sort of preliminary to the school.

I left the last Friday for these parts & although I haven't settled down to work yet, there's no doubt tomorrow or Tuesday will settle that point.

There seems to be the usual 'wind up' amongst all the new arrivals & I've no doubt several of these will get those memorable letters after their name "R.T.U" (Returned to Unit, in this case for being Unfit for Training).

I can consider myself fairly lucky to have managed a school so near home, at the same time I would have preferred Cambridge or Oxford.

There are quite a few of our boys here and at No.17 OCB nearby. I don't think you would know those who I have seen - Montford is one known by name.

*Cpl Kirby went down south somewhere to a Reception Battalion - I haven't heard lately from him. Sergeant Jones of the Trench ….. (*can't read this word) *is at Ripon.*

Well Mr Beresford I hope you are keeping out of the way of Jerry & not looking for too many souvenirs in No Man's Land.

74

Cpl Lamont told me about 3 weeks ago that you were still O.K, he was <u>jolly</u> glad to say so too .... I hope this report will always be possible.

I missed the boys very much although I think this side of the channel is much more congenial. I have heard news from the Battalion now & again but not very much.

I will write you again as to my progress, in the meantime <u>would</u> like a word from you, if you can manage to spare the time. You see I happen to know what correspondence is out there. I'm writing this in a priceless place, "our Club", it's an old castle fitted up for Cadets.

This is merely to show that I haven't forgotten you & never will. One of the finest officers I've had in all my long experience in France. This isn't mere eyewash, I'm quite sincere.

I tender my best wishes for continued good luck during your stay on active Service and hope you get over here very soon,

Very sincerely, yours,

W. Chadwick.

103. (*undated*) 1ˢᵗ Corps School.

My dear Mother and Father,

I go back to the batt tomorrow, they are out in rest so you need not expect me in the line for about another week. We have ripping weather here. We go back in motor lorries tomorrow afternoon.

I will write you later, I hope you are all very fit.
Your loving son,
Jack.

104. 6ᵗʰ September 1918 The Battalion, France.

My dear Mother and Father,

We had a very bon night at the Corps school, a real old rag. We came back in lorries a few days ago, quite a nice run.

I had 3 of my best men knocked out the other day. We have advanced and are now in the Boche support line which he occupied before he pushed us back on 9ᵗʰ April. I expect You'll have heard about it all. We have got him very nearly down and out, next year will do it. You may expect me home in about 8 weeks from now, at least I will be sweating by then.

We are having great weather and I am very fit and well at present, you wouldn't recognise me, I think I've grown a bit and got thicker. Of the mob that came out with me (13 in all) there are just 3 of us now. The others are sick, killed, etc. I think we are going to be the lucky ones so don't fidget.

Our divisional concert party had a smack in the eye lately, some of them were boiling what they thought was water in a petrol tin, but it wasn't and some are now in hospital.

I will write you again later, best of luck to you all,
Jack.

P.S. How is Uncle George & Auntie getting on and Auntie Beattie & Uncle Dick.

105. 8th September 1918 France.

My dear Mother and Father,

I go up tonight.

Best of luck to you all.
Your loving son,
Jack.

P.S. We had a battalion boxing show last night, it went A1.

106. 9th September 1918   The Line (German).

My dear Mother and Father,

We have got the old man on the run up here. He is back two or 3 miles already.

Have been wandering all over the Bosch line today, not very much in the way of souvenirs but I expect to send a parcel full home next time out. It seems very funny wandering over the old No Man's Land of a little while back, when I spent many hours crawling about it.

I have got a fine little German egg bomb, no bigger than a hen's egg and
76

black. I found a packet of candles of his which we are now using in this shack.

I have a pair of his boots they come half up your leg (the same as in that little book I sent you a little while back).

It is very wet and muddy up here, just our luck although we can't really grumble. If I remember I will send some of his and some of our barbed wire home when we come out. You will know what barbed wire really is then.

We have found iron plates in his line that he used to use for sniping through. The enclosed came out of one of his dugouts.

We are all very cheery, hope you at home all are the same. I may get leave December, don't expect me before.

I will write again tomorrow.
Your loving son,
Jack.

107.   10th September 1918

My dear Mother and Father,

We are getting on in fine style. I am very fit and well. I went in some dugouts today that used to be a German Coy H.Q., jolly fine place with beds and a glass window, jolly cosy, stove in one corner.

Will write more later.
Your loving son,
Jack.

108.   11th September 1918

My dear Mother and Father,

We are having a pretty wet time up here, it is very muddy but not too bad. I am now in a German pill box, very comfortable. We have 6 beds in the place, a couple of tables etc. The place was mined but the engineers removed it.

I got your letter of the 6th Mother dear & was very glad to get it.

I hope you are all fit and well.
Your loving son,
Jack.

109. 13th September 1918 France.

My dear Mother and Father,

Thanks very much for the two letters it was quite an event getting one from both of you. I am glad things are going on well at home.

I am back out of front line again and not doing so badly in the once Boche front line. Where we were before was rather wet, liquid mud about 1 foot deep in most places and the Boche in the same trench, we had a bombing fight one night and the next day he chucked perfectly good cigars over. They are Saxons in front of us.

Enclosed is another shoulder strap.

I have nothing much to tell you, at least I am unable to. We are in sight of and very nearly in a certain large town on a certain canal, that I can't name. *(Probably La Bassèe).*

Best of luck to you all,
Jack.

P.S. Does Uncle George still think we are losing.

110. 16th September 1918

My dear Mother and Father,

Thanks very much for your letters, but I wish you would not keep talking about leave, it will come in good time and if you keep thinking about it will seem much longer, besides I am not ready for it yet.

We are having a very bon war at present and resting at present in the old German front line.

John Darroch has got a job at Brigade H.Q. at present and the old skipper has just come back from a course.

Best of luck to you all,
Jack.

111. 17th September 1918 France.

My dear Mother and Father,

Everything still going strong I am very fit and well and we are having great weather.

78

About that photo, it is just imagination about not having had proper sleep. I had had just on 3 weeks rest when that was taken.

I saw an air fight this morning, one of our planes dived down at a Boche and drove him down.

Your loving son,
Jack.

112. 18th September 1918

My dear Mother and Father,

I had a letter from Syd yesterday. He is still going strong and is joining next year. Bill is getting on now for a certificate. (*Waldecker brothers from Bedford School*).

Well I am A1 and still going strong. I spent the whole day yesterday going round the old Boche line looking for souvenirs. Found another rifle, his latest pattern, I will try and bring it home with me.

Jack.

113. 19th September 1918

My dear Mother and Father,

Yes I have been in the German line for a long while now, we have got him moving now. He has held these old positions since 1914. We can see all of La B_____ (*confirms the town mentioned is La Bassée*) now and nearly up to it.

(*See poem at end of this letter "The Road to La Bassée"*).

You seem to have been enjoying yourself a bit lately. How are the two nippers getting on. What does the old Wink think of the swimming.

I shall be back in rest before this letter reaches you.

Cheerio,
Your loving son,
Jack

Sixteen years after the Great War, in 1934, Bernard Newman and Harold Arpthorp, two British veterans, together wrote this very poignant poem, for which they are to be thanked for bringing this sector of the Line to life again:-

"The Road to La Bassée".

I went across to France again, and walked about the line,
The trenches have been all filled in - the country's looking fine.
The folks gave me a welcome, and lots to eat and drink,
Saying, 'Allo, Tommee, back again? Ow do you do? In ze pink?'
And then I walked about again, and mooched about the line;
You'd never think there'd been a war, the country's looking fine.
But the one thing that amazed me most shocked me, I should say-e
There's buses running now from Bethune to La Bassée!

I sat at Shrapnel Corner and tried to take it in,
It all seemed much too quiet, I missed the war time din.
I felt inclined to bob down quick – Jerry sniper in that trench!
A minnie coming over! God, what a hellish stench!
Then I pulled myself together, and walked on to La Folette -
And the cows were calmly grazing on the front line parapet.
And the kids were playing marbles by the old Estaminet -
Fancy kiddies playing marbles on the road to La Bassée!

You'd never think there'd been a war, the country's looking fine -
I had a job in places picking out the old front line.
You'd never think there'd been a war - ah, yet you would, I know,
You can't forget those rows of headstones every mile or so.
But down by Tunnel Trench I saw a sight that made me start,
For there, at Tourbieres crossroads - a gaudy ice-cream cart!
It was hot, and I was dusty, but somehow I couldn't stay -
Ices didn't seem quite decent on the road to La Bassée.

Some of the sights seemed more than strange as I kept marching on.
The Somme's a blooming garden, and there are roses in Peronne.
The sight of dear old Arras almost made me give three cheers;
And there's kiddies now in Plugstreet, and mamselles in Armentiers.
But nothing that I saw out there so seemed to beat the band,
As those buses running smoothly over what was No Man's Land.
You'd just as soon expect them from the Bank to Mandalay,
As to see those buses running from Bethune to La Bassée.

Then I got into a bus myself, and rode for all the way,
Yes, I rode inside a bus from Bethune to La Bassée.

Through Beuvry and through Annequin, and then by Cambrin Tower -
The journey used to take four years, but now it's half an hour.
Four years to half an hour - the best speedup I've met,
Four years? Aye, longer still for some - they haven't got there yet.
Then up came the conductor chap, 'Vos billets s'il vous plait'.
Fancy asking for your tickets on the road to La Bassée.

Yes, I wondered what they'd think of it, those mates of mine who died.
And I wondered what they'd think of it - those mates of mine who died -
They never got to La Bassée, though God knows how they tried.
I thought back to the moments when their number came around,
And now those buses rattling over sacred, holy ground,
Of those buses rattling over the old pave close beside.
'Carry on that's why we died!' I could almost hear them say,
To keep those buses always running from Bethune to La La Bassée.

114. 21ˢᵗ September 1918 German Line.

My dear Mother and Father,

We are very fit and well, everything going A1. At present it is damned near open warfare we are fighting as we have now cleared Jerry's first system of defence and there is a gap of a mile or so to meet his next system of defence. In this area there are a few strong points with belts of wire about 20 yards deep round them, also a few pill boxes.

My platoon has dug little slits about 6 foot long and 3 feet deep in which they lie, we are very comfortable and fit and everyone is in great form, especially as Jerry is going under so quickly. We have never been on this ground since 1914 and now he is gradually falling back from it.

We have got little bivvies (shelters) in the bottom of a deep dried up ditch. It is quite a sporting life, especially as the old Boche does not know where we are, you see all our positions are camouflaged.

Today we have been sending crowds of little white propaganda balloons over Johnny. Four of our fighter planes having nothing to do, began diving at one and firing, they soon put it out, it was damned funny watching.

I am awfully fit now. I have not even got a coat up with me yet I am very warm at night. I have a sandbag of souvenirs with me, but I seem to lose them as quick as I get them as we are constantly on the move.

Best of luck to you all,
Jack.

115. 25ᵗʰ September 1918

Now out in rest and very fit, will write later. That shoulder strap with M W means Minenwerfer (trench mortar).

Jack.
(*Must have been v busy or tired as that was all in this unusually brief letter*).

116. 27ᵗʰ September 1918

My dear Mother and Father,

I am afraid you will be wondering why I have not written lately but I have been very busy. We are having a ripping time at this place.

Our billet is a.1. We all live in a civvy house and I am on a bed. There is proper furniture in our mess including a carpet, armchairs, stove, tables and white dinner cloth. There are no civvies in the place. The centre of the place has been completely smashed in.

Well cheerio,
Jack.

117. 28ᵗʰ September 1918 France.

My dear Mother and Father,

We are having a bon time out here lately. Two of us were away all day on Thursday, we set out in the morning and lorry jumped to _____. It took us about 3 hours to get there.

I have been bathing each day here. They are fine open-air baths but getting cold now. We had a relay race today. Our company is Y Company. We won by about 15 yards, 6 men a side, I swam.

I went to the theatre last night, it was a damn fine show, quite like old times only almost better. The troops are in wonderful spirits now.

Well the best of luck to you all at home.
Your loving son,
Jack.

118. 1ˢᵗ October 1918

My dear Mother and Father,

I am back again in the old front line again and very comfortable too.

Yesterday a platoon went forward to take a German post. They crawled down a drain and on the way they found the Boche garrison of 15 men sitting with

82

their bundles already to be taken prisoner. The old Boche had seen our fellows start and evidently thought it a good chance to get away. They are not all like that, the only exception though are his Storm troops, most of his ordinary troops are rotten.

What do you think of Bulgaria, not too bad is it. (*Bulgaria asked the Allies for an armistice which was signed on 29th September 1918. They had suffered 300,000 casualties including 100,000 killed, the most severe per capita of any country involved in the war*).

I have 2 rather nice rifles down at transport lines. They are being cleaned up to take home if I can when I come back on leave (two months time).

Well the very best of luck to you all. I expect you are all very cheery now, at any rate if you are half as cheery as the fellows in the line out here you won't be doing badly. I don't mean those damned base wallahs and people on soft jobs out here that come home with umpteen chevrons up and plenty of yarns to tell and never seen the line.

I expect the theatres were A1, do you good. Auntie seems to be having a pretty rotten holiday doesn't she.

Chambers has not sailed yet. There is a bit of a delay over commissions now.

Cheerio,
Your loving son,
Jack.

119. **2nd October 1918**

My dear Mother and Father,

I am fine and fit and we are doing A.1. Nothing to tell you at present.

I hope you are all going strong. I suppose you are still worrying are you not Mother dear. It is silly of you, I thought you would be used to it now. You will be quite hardened to it by the time Eric comes out.

Well best of luck to you,
Jack.

This is the last letter received. Jack was shot in the shin probably on 4th October. No names are recorded, but Z Company had 4 officers wounded that day. He was probably wounded during the attack at Don, which is on the La Bassée canal to Lille (about 8 miles to the north east) & about 4 miles east of La Bassée.

In letter no. 117 of 28.09.18 he says he was in Y Company, so the exact details of his final action are a little uncertain.

Jack was shot by a machine gunner in broad daylight in the shin. He was carried to safety in a brave move. After he returned home he was sent to Fowey to recuperate. There he borrowed a dinghy and rebuilt his strength by rowing it in the estuary and along the coast. He couldn't sleep in a bed for a while so slept on the floor and was for a long time ready to attack anyone moving in his bedroom after dark, for example his parents, which he apparently did on one occasion! His son John remembers Jack recounting tales about The Line, often whilst walking the dogs at night in the 1950s & 60s without any bitterness or apparent anguish.

Copy of letter written by Jack Beresford to Pandora Beresford, dated 4ᵗʰ October 1977.

(Pandora is Jack's third and youngest daughter).

Dearest Pandora,

You ask me what was life in the trenches like in the 1914-1918 War, that is hard to answer because life varied so much. Sometimes we'd be only 25 to 30 yards from the German trenches, in other parts of the front up to 3 - 400 yards was the No Man's Land. We were always expected by the "Brass Hats" at the base to dominate No Man's Land. Often very unrewarding and rather fruitless, especially so in winter time when one was wet, cold, hungry and tired and frightened for it is only then that real soldiering begins, - any fool can soldier when he is well fed, warm, rested and surrounded by friends.

Now to go on.

Just 12 weeks after I became an officer I went to France straight to "The Front" as it was called. I took a draft of 40 A3 boys (18 year olds) of the Cameron Highlanders up to join my regiment in the Line. On the 9ᵗʰ April 1918 the second great German offensive started and after 10 days fighting 4 of my draft were left. We fought on bully beef biscuits and the odd tot of rum. Virtually no sleep. I came out with a beard!

Right up to August we always expected another attack, for 5 weeks I never undressed and daily one went through anti-lousing drill, killing the little blighters off. Now normal trench life in the marshes round Festubert and Givenchy and the Craters was roughly like this. 6 days rest about 8 miles behind the line meant nearly every night going up on carrying parties, rations for the men in the line, wiring, trench digging getting shelled in the process most of the nights, machine gunned too. During the day we got some sleep.

Then the turn in the line meant 4 days in the reserve trenches on LINE, 4 days in close support of the front line, then 4 days in the front line in breast works or shell hole posts 120 to 200 yards apart, with little barbed wire out in front. Officers had to patrol the posts more or less continuously or be out in No Man's Land on patrol. Blackened faces and hands and wearing special crawling suits of brown canvas armed with a trench knife, knobkerry and bombs. It was a tough life up all night, then after dawn stand-to we'd get some grub down our necks and then after the posting of sentries the others would get some sleep in little shelters if they were lucky - behind the line and some parts there were rat infested cellars in ruined cottages. During the term of duty in the front line the officers would do 2 hours on and 4 off for the whole of the four days, that is if things were quiet.

At night the Germans used to send up star shells and Very Lights all night. If none went up that meant trouble and every man "stood to" ready.

Minenwerfer or minnies, as we call them, (trench mortar bombs) were a nightly curse and a hell of a mess they made of our defences at times. When they were fired they left a trail of red sparks until they reached their highest point, then nothing, but one knew roughly where there were going to fall and pushed off out of the way accordingly. Tiring and rather boring, for one gets used to that way of life. You know I was in the line for over 6 months and never a cold; fighting wearing the kilt had some advantages. We never suffered from mustard gas like trousered Tommies did. Gas was an awful bugbear, especially when they put over tear gas and your eyes just streamed. Then you ran into Phosgene or Yellow Grass gas (mustard), wearing respirators was very trying and seeing was difficult but I won't go on with that.

During nights all men would be on the alert with sentries posted forward in shell holes. You know in those days a lieutenant's life was reckoned to be roughly 14 days. I was lucky and did six and a half months. Towards the end of the war we had to attack and cross a canal in daylight, that bit of stupidity by the Brass Hats behind the Line cost my company in 3 days hefty casualties. We went in with 3 officers and 87 men came out with one officer and 15 men and that 4 weeks before the Armistice. One learnt to become a fatalist. I firmly believed they'd never hit me. If you didn't adopt that mentality you'd crack up. Well machine gunners got me in the end.

I hope this will give you some idea of fun and games in France.
Lots of love,
Your Dad.

P.S. Enclosed are some rough notes, if you can read them you are a genius!

Dad

Extra points taken from "rough notes".

- Commissioned to Liverpool Scottish, 1st Battalion, 55th division.
- Battle of the Somme 1918. (Bethune area of Flanders near French Belgian border) around Festubert, Givenchy, & The Craters.
- Marshy area and trenches when filled with water when 1 or 2 feet deep, so breastworks have to be constructed.
- Food mostly bully beef and biscuits, chlorinated water in petrol cans, sometimes meat cooked and ready cut up, brought up in sandbags. Rum ration issued in times of imminent attack, if you were lucky.
- Snipers on both sides and unsafe to show yourself in daylight.
- During the day in parts of the line we slept in cellars (rat infested) in wrecked villages, but most of the time one had to take the weather and make the best of it.

- Patrols out in No Man's Land every night over ground pitted with shell holes, dead bodies, rank grass and weeds in summer time. Dykes and ditches filled with barbed wire with duckboard bridges here and there.
- Fighting Patrols. Ours, usually 1 officer and 8 men or our other patrols 1 officer and 2 to 3 men. The kilt left behind so special crawling suits of brown canvas, faces and hands blackened and wearing a wool balaclava cap.
- German Patrols. 20 to 40 men, mostly Bombers.

List of souvenirs sent home, as recorded in his letters.

1. 4th April 1918
German Very Light pistol. 2 clips of cartridges in German Housewife.

2. 5th April 1918
Bought 2 French caps (artillery & infantry) for 5fr 50c.

3. 22nd April 1918
Boche cap & bullets, French respirator & Flying Corps cap, piece of shell that hit me without effect and revolver. I doubt parcel will reach you, but I am chancing it. Just snaffled a Boche Very Light pistol & fine fuse cap. Endless souvenirs here if you can carry them.

4. 28th April 1918
Prussian Guard cap (black & white), German bible 'The Christian Soldier' (with picture of Christ & behind him a burning cottage), 2 shoulder straps of the 301st regiment, some German tobacco. Each State has a different coloured button (Bavaria is red & black, etc). Souvenir spoon of B_____. (Betune?).

5. 11th May 1918
On patrol this morning came across dead Boche. Found Iron Cross, 1st Class on him. Took a few buttons, his shoulder strap & ID disc. Belonged to 362nd Jaeger Regiment. Enclosed is ribbon.

6. 16th May 1918
German pack made of cow skin, German gas mask, water bottle, bayonet, buttons & French buttons. German fuse caps (quite safe), tobacco & round tin with pepper in it. All from men in 362nd regiment, 4th Ersatz Division in their attack on 9th April. Pack from a private of the 1st Guards Reserve regiment.

7. 27th May 1918
Enclosed is the identification Disc of the German from whom I took the Iron Cross: J.R.362: Jaeger Regiment 362 / 22.3.91 is his Date of birth / Heitum Sylt is the name of the place where his home is. (Heitum is a village on North Sea Island of Sylt, Schlesweig Holstein).

8. 28th May 1918
German steel helmet & ground sheet (Eric can use for camping & can be rigged up as a little tent). (Drawing in the letter shows how to use it as a tent.). Taken from a Private of the 4th Guards Reserve Division the last time I was up.

9. 29th May 1918
German tin hat, shrapnel ball, French & German bullet & case, cartridge I used to fire the 6 inch gun. Take about 8 days to get home. Please keep a record of all these things I send home, number them and keep a little book with all the information about them. Perhaps Vera (sister) would like to do it.

10. 8th July 1918
Paper packet to put in German tin, shoulder strap, great coat button. Scarlet Pimpernels from no man's land.
Boche tin hat, belt, ammunition pouches, 'potato masher' (stick-bomb).

11. 17th July 1918
Boche tin hat, equipment belts and pouches and cap, French cap and English black lachrymatory (tear gas goggles). Also a handkerchief case with the divisional Rose (*55th Division*) on it for you Mother dear. Also photo of my batman, a great Irishman and as broad a brogue as possible and as cute as they make them.

12. 1st July 1918
2 rather nice rifles down at transport lines. They are being cleaned up to take home if I can when I come back on leave (two months' time).

Locations from his letters.

8th April 1918
(Betune?) B_____ about 5.5km from billet.

13th April 1918
_____ canal. (*La Bassée?*).

10th May 1918
See location of Route A Keep, near Festubert.

26th June 1918
15th Platoon, Z coy, 1st Liverpool Scottish.

10th July 1918
Westminster Bridge.

4th August 1918
At a place called by the same name as the famous Hall at home, where the German Officers live.

3rd September 1918
Our push at G_____ (*Givenchy?*).

13th September 1918
We are in sight of and very nearly in a certain large town on a certain canal (*La Bassée?*).

19th September 1918
La B_____. (*La Bassée is confirmed*).

Part Two

Jack Beresford – A life

(With his kind permission this is based on an article entitled 'Rugby's Loss – Rowing's Gain" by John Jenkins drawn from his article for MARS & MINERVA, The Journal of The Special Air Service. Incorporating the Journals of the Special Air Service Regimental Association and The Artist Rifles Association. Vol 11 No. 2. December, 2006. Reorganised and added to by John Beresford for this book).

Introduction.

In sculling boat Jack Beresford looking over his shoulder. 1920s

Master oarsman, ruthless competitor, a national icon for gold in his fifth Olympic Games. Sounds familiar?

There are comparatively few pictures, still or moving of Jack Beresford, the most accomplished oarsman in Olympic history before Sir Steve Redgrave. Most of these show him crouched over oars, winning or having just won, another race at an Olympic regatta or under the Henley sun. Few show the stocky figure, the slightly dumpy legs supporting a broad and powerful upper body, the generous grin, high cheekbones and neatly parted blond hair.

His racing weight was a little over 11 stone and he was about 5 foot 10 inches tall (when Redgrave carried the British flag at Atlanta, he was over 16 stone), so his achievements were all the more remarkable in that he was basically a lightweight oarsman at a time when this category was not recognised.

As a giant of British sport between the wars he loses nothing to Fred Perry, Walter Hammond or Dixie Dean. He was a classic Corinthian sporting hero.

British oarsman, Jack Beresford competed in five consecutive Olympics between 1920 and 1936 winning five medals, three gold and two silver. He was Champion Sculler of Great Britain for seven consecutive seasons from 1920. At Henley, then still the world's premier annual regatta, he won the Diamond Sculls four times as well as all five principal events at Henley. He remains one of the most illustrious rowing champions in history and enjoyed a remarkably long career. It is almost certainly only the cancellation of the 1940 Games in Tokyo that prevented a sixth appearance.

Chapter One: Early Days

Jack Beresford was born on 1st January 1899 in London, the eldest of three children (Eric born 1905 and Ethal Vera born 1906). His father, Julius 'Berry' Beresford Wiszniewski was born in 1868 in Middlesex and married Ethel Mary Wood in 1897. He changed their surname to just Beresford in 1914.

Berry's father, Julius Bernard Wiszniewski was born in 1833 and emigrated from Danzig (Gdansk was the Polish name, but became Danzig after Poland was annexed by the Kingdom of Prussia in 1793). It is reported that he was taken to England by his governess aged 12, in 1845 and possibly the name Beresford came from her, but that is uncertain.

Berry's father married Stella Louisa Davey in Tewkesbury in 1866. They had six children (Stella Beatrice, Julius, Louisa Franziska, Bernard Stanley, Bernard Granville and Pardia (Peter, known in this book as Uncle Pandy).

(Genealogical research with thanks to Roma Beresford, Michael Beresford's late wife. Michael is Eric's son and also an Olympic oarsman).

Stella Beatrice married Richard Hicks in 1896 and he and Berry formed the partnership Beresford & Hicks, makers of fine furniture including reproduction antiques with offices and showroom in Curtain Road, London and a factory in Hoxton.

Father & Son, J Beresford Snr and Jnr (Berry and Jack). 1925

Berry was a notable oarsman who had won an Olympic silver medal in the British coxed IV in 1912 as well as several notable wins at Henley. He went on to become a very well respected and successful coach.

In 1903 they moved to "Belfairs", 19 Grove Park, Chiswick which was built in 1898, one of the largest in The Grove complex with coach house and stables. An English Heritage Blue Plaque was unveiled in 2005 by his son John, to commemorate Jack Beresford by marking the place that remained his home until 1940. This was the first blue plaque ever awarded to a rower.

The Blue Plaque. 2005

Jack attended Bedford School between 1913 and 1917 and it was here that he developed his sporting prowess. He always said that rugby was his first love

1st XV, Bedford School. 1917

above rowing. He captained the 1st XV Rugby team where, as a front row forward and pack leader, he was known as "The Tank". He was picked as an England Schoolboy International, although no games were played officially between 1914 and 1921 as all fixtures were cancelled by the Rugby Football Union nine days after declaration of war in August 1914. All players were encouraged to enlist.

Crescent House IV, Bedford School. 1917

Names of the IV:
K S Robertson   E H Hime
J Beresford   C P Hausser   S R Schofield

German Prisoners act in a concert at Bedford School. 1917
D I Coates   J H S Fea   J Beresford

One tale of Jack's Bedford days, recounted below, was handwritten by him into his photo album. It reveals a lot about the impact of the war on the school – and Jack's own sense of fun.

Jack was playing a German prisoner of war in a sketch entitled *"Hear the Haughty Heads of Houses Howl the Hunnish Hymn of Hate!"* It was part of a concert in aid of the Public Schools Hospital that took place on 31st March 1917.

This is how he described what happens next:

After the concert Halsey (who had come in uniform) marched Fea & I down into the town. We were wearing German uniform. The Night Patrol passed us in the Avenue but luckily did not notice us as all lights were shaded. On coming into the High Street a crowd quickly collected and followed us. We slouched along in the gutter muttering what German we knew, while Halsey marched behind cursing us. He told the people that we had escaped from the Duke of Bedford's Estate at Ampthill and that we were being marched back to HQ.

On turning down Mill Street we picked up a lot of Tommies so Fea and I began talking about Hindenburg and saying that the Englishers would be beaten. That rubbed them up and some of the Tommies wanted to mob us, so we shut up for a bit and incidentally got the wind up properly. However, Halsey promptly ticked them off and they dried up and got quite friendly. Then one of them asked Halsey if he could help in getting us up to HQ. So old Halsey said "Good god no, I have been wounded 4 times, the last on the Somme, I am used to these devils and now my job is looking after German prisoners". On turning up into St Peter's Street some officers came up to Halsey but he took no notice and promptly wheeled us into the Incubator gate (The Prep School).*

As we turned into the gate Halsey told a sergeant that he was taking us up to Headquarters in de Parys Avenue, and wanted to avoid the crowd, so would he stop them from coming through. However, while he was speaking to the sergeant Fea and I slipped off. Then Halsey turned round and seeing us oiling off came after us with great yells.

We rushed home as hard as we could. I went across the field to the House while Fea and Halsey cut off to Mr Czanne's. I was in bed jolly quickly that night.

About 15 minutes later the alarm had been given that two Germans had escaped into the school grounds and were in hiding somewhere near the new Laboratories. The night patrol came up and searched the Labs, then they came up to the school and the officer in charge asked Walton, the school porter, if he had heard anything about two Germans escaping. However Walton twigged what was on and said nothing to him.

Then the Military Police drew a cordon round the whole school grounds, while a crowd patrolled the streets on bicycles without lights. These men were kept out searching till after 12 o'clock.

The Special Constables and civil police were also out on the job and were detailed to form a cordon round Chief's (Headmaster's) *garden. This was told me by Mrs Chief who had been told by the Chief of Police.*

In the meanwhile the A.P.M. had heard that the prisoners had escaped from the school grounds by climbing over the walls and going through the Moravian girls school, and thence to Goldington. Accordingly he took a party out in a car and searched out there till 1 o'clock (April 1ˢᵗ).

(This from Major Hilton, Brigade major). The sentries outside the different battalion Headquarters challenged everybody coming along. The A.P.M. was very sick about it when he heard next day and was ragged a great deal by the officers as he was not exactly popular.

Whilst at Bedford, Jack served in the Officer Training Corps from September 1913 to April 1917. It's interesting to note that he attempted to enlist in 1916 but his father sent him back to school until 1917, the year he turned 18.

He joined the Regiment in May 1917, (regimental number 765670). He attended No 4 OCB, Oxford from 4th August to 27th November 1917 and was commissioned through the 2nd Battalion Artists Rifles on 28th November 1917 to the 10th (Territorial) Battalion The Liverpool Scottish.

It is not known why he joined the Artists. Perhaps he was aware of them being one of the elite Territorial units in London or he may have read of their outstanding rugby record. It's possible he may have played for one of the Public Schools XVs against the Artists in the series of recruiting matches organised by Colonel Shirley during the 1916 season. He would almost certainly have played rugby for the Artists Rifles during his training, so this would have been the last game of rugby that he played.

He was posted to 3rd (Reserve) Battalion of the Liverpool Scottish at Park Hall camp between Oswestry and Gobowen. This was the training and holding battalion for the 1st/10th and the 2nd/10th Battalion which were the Liverpool Scottish Battalions on active service in France and Flanders.

Jack never forgot his old school, Bedford. Following the 1936 Berlin Olympics all Gold medal winners were presented with an oak sapling, known as a Hitler Oak. Jack donated his to the school, where it flourished until it had to be felled for the building of a new Recreation Center which opened in 1980. In a letter to the Daily Telegraph of 22nd September 2006, Martin Humphrys, Thames Regional Rowing Council and former Master in Charge of Rowing wrote:-

Before being felled the Biology Department took cuttings and the young saplings were planted throughout the school estate and at the school's nature reserve.

The then bursar, Major Donald Mantell, himself a former member of the school's Boat Club and first VIII, ensured that the wood from the oak was made into planks for the specific use of the Boat Club and only released on his authority. Thus, successive generations of oarsmen have seen the Hitler oak made into bowshields for those young men and their coaches at the school who had achieved success at both national and international level. All shields carry information on the back to indicate they are part of the Hitler oak and signed by the Master in Charge of the day. I am not sure if any of the wood is left but the little oaks have been able to flourish and more importantly the spirit of Beresford lives on.

One example of where the timber was used, was to make a bowshield for silver medal winners Abraham and Pinkney at the National Schools Regatta in 1989. They went on to win the Home International junior pairs.

In further tribute to Jack's achievements, the "Jack Beresford Games Room" was named at Pemberley Boarding House, where Jack, his brother Eric, his nephew Michael and son John all boarded and rowed for the school. Michael

Hitler Oak planting at Bedford School. 1936

Beresford opened this on the 150th anniversary of the Boat Club in 2011. John remembers:

I was able to give this room my Father's oar from the 1916 1ˢᵗ VIII, inscribed with the crew members and victory over Shrewsbury. Also presented were framed photos from when he was Captain of the 1ˢᵗ XV and Captain of Boats. Perhaps one day they will be given his 1916 1ˢᵗ VIII blazer, which I wore in 1963 and 1964 when rowing in the 1ˢᵗ VIII and still wear on suitable rowing occasions, despite it being over 100 years old.

Chapter Two: The Infantry

The Liverpool Scottish was correctly known as the 10th (Scottish) Battalion, The King's (Liverpool Regiment) TF (standing for Territorial Force). It had been part of the Territorial Force before the war, having been formed in 1908 from the 8th (Scottish) Volunteer Battalion of the King's (formed in 1900). The 8th Battalion had been formed in 1900 in response to the Boer War. On the outbreak of war in 1914, a second battalion of the 10th was formed, hence 1st\10th and 2nd/10th and subsequently the 3rd/10th which was formed in May 1915. The 1st/10th went to France and Flanders in November 1914, one of the first territorial battalions to do so. The 2nd/10th went across in February 1917. In spring 1918 during the general manpower crisis the 1st/10th and 2nd/10th combined on active service to form one battalion, which is mentioned in one of Jack's letters.

Jack went to France on 3rd April in 1918, aged only 19 and served as Platoon Commander Z Coy 1st/10th Battalion the Liverpool Scottish. As an officer in Z Coy he would have been close to Lt Basil Rathbone MC, later the dashing film star and Shakespearean actor, who also acted in many other plays and films, including playing Sherlock Holmes in the 14 Hollywood films produced between 1939-46.

The Liverpool Scottish had several well-known rugby players in their ranks before and during the war, especially associated with the Liverpool & Birkenhead Park RUFCs and including several internationals. Two officers, Fred Turner, captain of Scotland in 1914 and "Toggie" Kendall, captain of England in 1903 were killed within a few days of each other in January 1915 and both are buried in Kemmel churchyard.

From May 1918 55th division and the Liverpool Scottish held the line in the Givenchy sector until the beginning of October when the Germans started withdrawing. Jack's Uncle Pandy had been wounded in the same sector, Givenchy, on 9th April 1918 when they were pushed back by the German Spring Offensive.

His company was involved in a nasty attack at Don, south-west of Lille and on the canal near La Bassée in early October, suffering heavy casualties. It was almost certainly during this attack that he was badly wounded in the shin by machine-gun fire as 4 officers are recorded in the War Diary of the Liverpool Scottish as being wounded that month, although they are not named. Other sources have reported that he was wounded the day before the Armistice but this cannot be so as the War Diary records no combat on that day, though they were an advanced guard battalion.

The final advance took the Battalion eastwards south of Lille, then passed Tournai and at the Armistice they were further east of Tournai at Ath in

Belgium. Jack was promoted to Lieutenant on 28th May 1919. His son John recalls:

In later years I recall how Father often talked about his experiences in the trenches while walking the family dogs during dark winter months. I think he did actually enjoy the excitement mixed at times with fear. After the war? I don't know, perhaps that's why he immersed himself in rowing. Certainly, he would talk to me about being out in No Man's Land and life in the Line without any apparent anguish or resentment. Perhaps, because he didn't hide his experiences, like many others did, that was his way of coping. I found it fascinating and will always remember.

His war wound prevented him from playing rugby again, so instead he took up rowing whilst recuperating at Fowey where he had a rowing boat to scull and gradually built up his strength again.

Jack Beresford at Fowey, Cornwall, in rowing boat. 1919

Chapter Three: After the War

Following his demobilization in 1919, Jack returned to London and joined Beresford & Hicks, his father's furniture manufacturing business and Thames Rowing Club where his father had been a member since 1904 having moved from Kensington Rowing Club to get a higher level of competition.

Thames presented the book shown below to Berry, his father, in gratitude for all that he had given to his Club, including coaching to produce many winning crews.

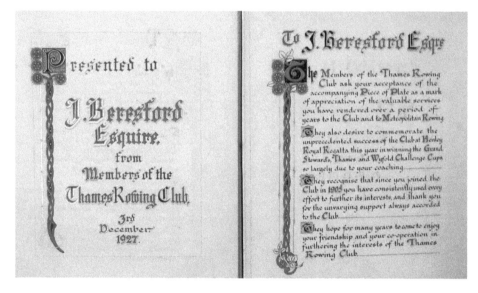

Book presented to J Beresford snr, Berry, by Thames Rowing Club. 1927

Jack was racing again in 1919 and was at Royal Henley Peace Regatta. The official programme shows his father at stroke and J.Beresford jnr, as he was known, as a substitute. The importance of the Peace Regatta, which will be commemorated by Henley Royal Regatta in 2019, was spelt out by Sir Steve Redgrave, Chairman of the Regatta's Committee of Management. He said:

The 1919 Royal Henley Peace Regatta was a key milestone in the sport of rowing and was staged by the rowing community to help heal the wounds and hasten the return to normality of the Allied nations and their troops recovering from the First World War.

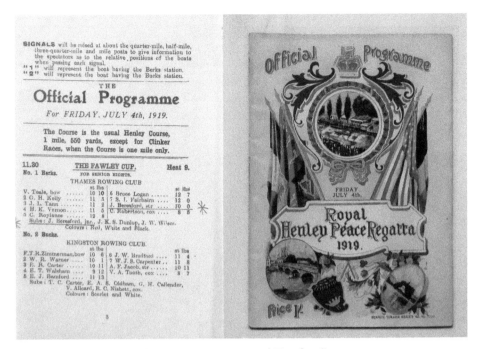

The Official Programme cover and Fawley Cup event. 1919

From the outset Jack displayed the brilliance of a winner and won the Wingfield Sculls, the Amateur Sculling Championship of Great Britain, seven times from 1920 to 1926.

The Bystander magazine of 28th July 1920 wrote the following article in their Sports & Pastimes section, which shows his brilliance as a sculler:

By supplementing his win in the Diamond Sculls at Henley by a convincing victory in the Wingfields last week, J Beresford, Jnr, has proved himself to be the best amateur sculler of the year. His father is the well-known veteran of the Thames Rowing Club who, although in his fifty third year, stroked the Thames Grand VIII at Henley this month. The son has of course, followed in his father's footsteps as an oarsman, but it only occurred to him to try his hand at sculling last year. It was a lucky inspiration, for most scullers are born not made and Beresford certainly is a born sculler; he has a nice easy action, plenty of pace and is a finished waterman.

At Henley Royal Regatta uniquely, he won all five principle events:-

The Diamond Sculls, open to the world, four times in 1920 and 1924 to 26.
The Silver Goblets and Nickalls Challenge Cup for coxless pairs with Gordon
      Killick in 1928 and 1929.
The Stewards Challenge Cup for IVs in 1932.
The Grand Challenge Cup for VIIIs in 1923 and 1928.
The Centenary Double Sculls in 1939. (See this story later).

In 1920 at the age of only 21, Jack made his mark internationally at the Antwerp Olympics (officially known as the Games of the VII Olympiad) in the Single Sculls. In a dramatic duel he lost to the American Champion Sculler, John B Kelly (known as Jack Kelly), by one second. This race has been described as one of the closest in Olympic history until the men's single sculls final at Rio in 2016 when Drysdale was given the race over Martin by five thousandths of a second.

Olympic Sculls final. 1920

The two Jacks later became good friends. Both had fought in WW1 in France and survived. Jack Kelly was also a sculling legend having won 126 straight races in single sculls in 1919-20, including Olympic Gold in single sculls in 1920 and double sculls in 1920 and 1924. Daniel J. Boyne's book, *"Kelly. A Father, a Son, an American Quest"* makes engrossing reading and has many references to Jack Beresford.

Jack Beresford won his first Olympic Gold in the single sculls in Paris in 1924. That year he also won the Philadelphia Gold Challenge Cup for the World Amateur title which he retained at Putney in 1925, beating the American Champion Sculler, Walter Hoover whom he had beaten in the Diamonds that year. Hoover had beaten him in the Diamond Sculls final in 1922.

A cutting from the Philadelphia Evening Telegraph below shows that Hoover had hoped to challenge him in 1926, but Beresford did not go to the USA.

The article also wrote about Hoover's training regime:-

The time was when Hoover held to a moderate level of training. But after his defeat by Beresford in the Diamond Sculls at Henley he learnt his lesson and began to go in for severe regimes.

While on the Thames training for Henley, Hoover noted that Beresford was on the river at all times. It seemed to the American that the English sculler lived on the course. When it came to the race Beresford was trained to the minute, while Hoover lacked something which he attributed to being short of work.

After the race Beresford kept right on rowing. So, Hoover decided that the Briton had the correct 'dope' after all and the American adopted the Beresford system.

'Hoover awaits Beresford' press cutting for
Philadelphia Gold Cup. 1926

The Philadelphia Gold Cup, known as The Gold Cup began in 1920, during the heyday of Philadelphia rowing, in memory of John B Kelly's (Jack Kelly's) first Olympic Gold Medal for the United States in the 1920 Olympics. The event pitted the best amateur male single scullers in the world against each other in a sprint race on the famed Schuylkill River course.

The contest and the cup disappeared in the early 1960s, only to re-emerge in 2011 after a 50-year hiatus. A private group of Philadelphia rowing enthusiasts rediscovered the Gold Cup and reinstated the event and tradition to its rightful place in single scull rowing prominence, with the positive expansion of the competition to women.

A stickler for fair play Jack Beresford lost a Diamonds Sculls final when his opponent hit the booms and stopped. He, being well ahead, also stopped for a 'fair race' but was unable to pick up his rhythm again and was beaten. He never made that mistake again. He became a ruthless but fair competitor.

'Jack Beresford signed photo in his sculling boat. 1927

Jack carried on with the family furniture business, trained ferociously and as captain of the Thames VIII won a silver medal at Amsterdam in 1928 behind the Americans. He switched to coxless IV, with three others of that Thames

'The Thames Rowing Club VIII signed photo incl 'Berry' as coach. 1928

The GB IV signed. 1932

VIII, for Los Angeles in 1932 winning gold in the American's backyard.

However, as well as competing in VIIIs, IVs and pairs he still sculled and won silver at the Empire Games in Hamilton, Ontario in 1930. Gold medalist was Bobbie Pearce of Australia with a Bronze for Fred Bradley of England, shown in the photo below. The second photo shows Jack Beresford and Ted Phelps who were Amateur and Professional Sculling Champions of the World.

Empire Games, Hamilton, 3 scullers (Bradley, Pearce, Beresford). 1930

World Amateur & Professional Sculling Champions, Beresford & Phelps. 1930

He was presented with a beautiful Canadian canoe by the Canadian Legion of Ontario. This canoe is still in use on the Thames today at Henley. The photo below shows the christening ceremony of 'Canadian Legion' at Putney, with many famous oarsmen afloat, including his father, recorded as 'Pater'.

Canoe christening at Putney with many rowing celebrities. 1931

Rowing celebrities from top left to lower right:

Metropolitan Police VIII; Walter Obernesser - Lightweight Champion Sculler; Ron Williams, Bill William, Pater; Jack Beresford (Owner of "Canadian Legion" canoe); Ernie Barry - Worlds Professional Champion 1912 – 1919; Ted Phelps - Worlds Professional Champion 1930 – 1931; Bob Pearce - World Amateur Champion 1928 – 1932

Chapter Four: The 1936 Berlin Olympics

The infamous Berlin Olympics in 1936 was intended by Hitler to show the might and supremacy of Germany. At the Opening Ceremony Jack Beresford carried the Union Flag leading the British Olympic Team into the stadium. He was also the British Rowing Team Captain.

Berlin Opening Ceremony, Jack Beresford GB Flag Bearer. 1936

He recounted stories of Nazi 'dirty tricks' to try to ensure their sporting supremacy. The mysteriously 'missing boat' tale is told below. He also described how Nazi soldiers marched at night, very noisily, outside the team sleeping quarters of foreign athletes.

There were other stories of the ways the Nazis tried to enhance their chances of winning, one of which is related in the wonderful book *"The Boys in the Boat"* by Daniel James Brown.

Brown tells the story of the VIIIs final where it was a foul wet day with a very strong gusty cross wind and in an extraordinary reversal of the normal rules when the fastest boats are given the favoured lanes, this year Germany and their Italian allies, with the slower times, were given the inside favoured lanes and the USA the most exposed and rough outside lane. However, against all the odds, USA won Gold with Italy second and Germany third, with only one second between the first three boats.

Also clips of the Cross Country equestrian event (available on YouTube) show that the Germans knew there was a deep hole in the water at the water jump, which they avoided, whereas foreign competitors tended to be unseated by their horses falling into the hole, sometimes reappearing with horses' noses festooned in weed!

Ref: YouTube:- *Leni Riefenstahl, 1936 Opening Ceremony. At 1.35 minutes see GB.*
Leni Riefenstahl, 1936 Olympic rowing. German IV & gold medal USA VIII.

Jack Beresford was 37, considered old for an Olympic rower, and though he and his partner in the double sculls, Dick Southwood, had trained relentlessly, the Germans were threatening to carry all before them.

Beresford and Southwood had one trump card. Germany had relied heavily on English professional coaches working in Germany and one of these, Eric Phelps, warned the British that unless they found a lighter, more slender boat they would have no chance. Within a week the boat was built. Within another it was tested, shipped off to Germany and lost deliberately, it is alleged. A mere couple of days before the games it was traced to a railway siding between Hamburg and Berlin and was ready in time for the regatta. Their eventual success was partly due to their rigorous training as well as

Beresford and Southwood's first and only outing in the new boat at Putney. 1936

Beresford and Southwood on the water at Berlin, picture post card. 1936

gamesmanship supervised by Eric Phelps. He told them, "The Germans are an 1800m crew. Stick with them that far and you'll beat them."

Michael Phelps whose family story can be read in Maurice Phelps fascinating book, *"The Phelps Dynasty: A story of a Riverside Family"*, generously gave this picture postcard to John Beresford at the Beresford Blue Plaque unveiling in 2005. Jack wrote to his mother the following on the reverse of the picture:

Dear Mother,
I thought you'd like to see that we're both still bearing up mighty well and fit we both are and hope to pull it off tomorrow. I was glad to have your last long letter and do hope Pater is better.
Your loving son,
Jack.

On finals day the German crowd, with Hitler present, were celebrating their fifth of five consecutive gold medals. In the next race the favourites for the Double Sculls, Willy Kaidel and Joachim Pirsch, showed every sign of making it six. They even featured on one of the German Olympic postage stamps.

At the start Southwood noticed that the Belgian umpire could not see all the crews when he raised his megaphone to his face. Knowing the Germans had jumped the gun in previous races he told Jack to watch them and he would start as soon as they did. That is exactly what happened!

What better way to find out what happened than by reading Beresford's own words. He was asked in 1964, by World Sports, the official magazine of the British Olympic Association, to be one of four gold medallists of the past to recall their greatest triumph. The other three were Anita Lonsbrough (1960

Women's 200 metres breaststroke) ; Harold Abrahams (1924, 100 metres sprint Gold, depicted in the film *"Chariots of Fire"* and also an Old Bedfordian); Harry Malin (1920 and 1924 Boxing Gold).

This is Jack's chosen story:

With blades almost clashing.

It was in the 1920 Olympics that I had my first lesson of race technique - beaten by John B Kelly (Jack Kelly) of the United States by one second for the gold medal in the sculls. That final made me decide to prepare for 1924 and I got my first gold medal in Paris. Four years later I was captain of the British VIII in Amsterdam and we won a silver medal behind the Americans. Then four of us in Thames Rowing Club got together for Henley, went to California for the 1932 Games and won gold in the coxwainless IVs.

In 1935 Dick Southwood teamed up with me in a double sculler - object Berlin, 1936. By that time we were both pretty tough and mature, with the confidence and will-to-win well ingrained in us. In those days there were no open double-sculling races in England, but with 10 months practice behind us and 2000 miles in the boat plus daily early-morning running and exercises, we were strong and fit.

In our first race in Berlin we met five other countries, including the Germans, European record- holders. They were very fast off the mark and their tactics were to get ahead and then edge over and "line" us up, i.e. scull dead in front of us, giving us their wash. They succeeded in doing that the first time and the other four countries were so much behind that the single umpire in the launch wasn't able to control the course of the two leaders. At the finish we had to ease up or we would have bumped them and damaged our boat. So we just smiled and made no comment after the race.

Next came the rêpechage heat, which we won very easily and so got back into the final. By then we had the "Indian sign" well and truly on those Germans, at least so we reckoned, and it worked out that way. In that final, besides Britain, were Germany, Poland, France, USA and Australia. We were determined to stay with those Germans but even at halfway (1000m) they led by 1½ lengths with the other countries out of the hunt.

At that point we challenged for the lead and went on doing so until they "blew up". We literally gained foot-by-foot for the next 800m until at 1800m we were dead level. And so we raced to the 1900m mark with blades almost clashing, for they had tried the old game of trying to line us up, but not again! Right in front of Hitler's box the Germans cracked and we went on to win by 2½ lengths.

The air was electric, for until we broke the spell Germany had won five finals off the reel. Yes, the last win in the doubles was the greatest and the sweetest, for we had come out to Berlin without a race and beaten the world.

Beresford and Southwood winners wreath ceremony. 1936

The drama of their race can be seen in the 1992 BBC series *"Tales of Gold"* narrated by Kenneth Branagh. Jack Beresford is one of the British Olympians featured in programme five. An amateur filmed the last part of this race but the actual moment of Pirsch blowing up is missed as the photographer, obviously assuming another German victory, had panned away over the excited crowd in the stand. Panning back to the race again, Beresford and Southwood were well ahead and had also changed lanes.

Hitler stormed out of his box in fury.

Jack always rowed under Thames Rowing Club colours and they still have a number of framed photographs of him on their Clubhouse walls. The 1936 Berlin Olympics oak leaf wreath that was presented to Beresford and Southwood when they won the double sculls was hanging at the Club for many years. It is now on permanent loan from Thames and displayed at The River and Rowing Museum, Henley. Many of Jack's medals are also displayed there.

Thames Rowing Club also have much memorabilia from Beresford and Southwood's victories including the bow of their Berlin double sculling boat and a sculling blade from the Centenary Double Sculls at Henley in 1939.

Chapter Five: *Life after the Olympics*

In 1939, Jack Beresford and Dick Southwood, the reigning Olympic champions entered a new event at Henley, the Centenary Double Sculls. The final resulted in a dead-heat between Beresford and Southwood and the Italian crew who were the European Champions. Perhaps the Stewards, aware of the strong headwind, took notice of Southwood being 33 and Beresford 40 years of age and did not order a re-row. Southwood's account is that Beresford had the presence of mind to approach the exhausted Italians in the boat tent, congratulate them and suggest a re-row. The Italians declined and all four men were awarded medals and silver cups.

Jack was not prepared to remain content with his splendidly won laurels. He felt it important to serve the sport that had allowed him so many triumphs. He coached the Cambridge crew of 1937 although not always successfully. On one occasion he provided them with a barrel of beer at the boathouse which it is said he insisted be finished before the race!

He served on the British Olympic Council from 1936 and was a member of the Organising Committee for the London Olympics of 1948 and also a rowing Selector from 1938 to 1954. He mentored the British double sculling partnership of Richard Burnell and Bert Bushnell who won gold. This is featured in the BBC film *"Bert and Dickie"* shown just before the 2012 London Olympics.

During the Second World War he was for a time a Metropolitan Police Special Constable before he moved from Chiswick. When he moved to Wargrave-on-Thames in 1940 he served in the 6th Royal Berkshire Home Guard, Twyford Battle and Defence Platoons, bringing back memories of 1918 in France.

He had wanted to enlist but his business was required for essential wartime production of such things as parts for the de Haviland DH 98 Mosquito aircraft, whose frame was constructed almost entirely of wood: It was nicknamed "The Wooden Wonder". They also made ammunition boxes, etc. He told stories of the Blitz in the East End of London and being on fire watch at their Hoxton factory, which did suffer bomb damage.

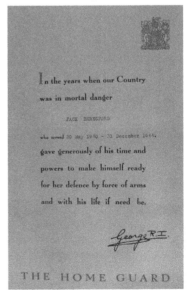

Home Guard certificate, Jack Beresford. 1944

He continued to involve himself in sport. A letter from him to The Crookes Laboratories, London, on behalf of The Organising Committee for the XIVth Olympiad, London 1948, shows his concern about British sportsmen's nutrition because of food rationing. He said that the winning Thames Rowing Club IV and Leander VIII had taken Crookes Vitamin Quota capsules throughout training for Henley and were anxious to continue with them right up to the Games.

He was Team Manager and part-time coach of the English crews in the Argentine and Uruguay in 1947 and of the English rowing team at the New

Empire Games, Lake Karapiro, New Zealand final of the VIIIs. 1950 Australia beat New Zealand by one foot with England 3rd.

Zealand Empire Games in 1950 and of the British rowing squad at the Helsinki Olympics of 1952.

He was elected a Henley Steward and umpire in 1946 and was on the council of the Amateur Rowing Association from 1932 to 1967 and later served as President of Thames Rowing Club.

A family man, he married Mary Leaning in 1940 in Chelsea Old Church with a Guard of Honour by two members of the famous Phelps Dynasty, Dick and Tom,

Wedding at Chelsea Old Church with Guard of Honour. 1940

116

both winners of the Doggett Coat and Badge. The church was blitzed on 16th March 1941 but was rebuilt after the war. They had a a daughter, Elizabeth and son, John. After they divorced he married Stroma Morrison in 1958 and had two daughters, Carina and Pandora.

As well as his rowing life, for many years he was managing director of the family business, Beresford & Hicks, in Curtain Road, London. He had a very good eye for design and they made furniture for amongst other places, Buckingham Palace, for which he received the Royal Warrant in 1958.

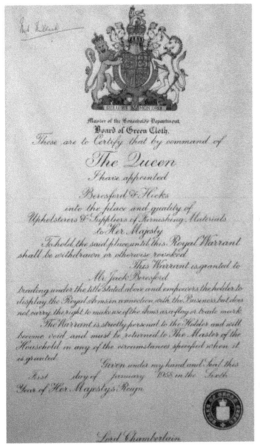

The Royal Warrant,
Beresford & Hicks. 1958

John Beresford writes:

My father was a fiercely patriotic Englishman who loved the Royal Family. He would not discuss his own Polish ancestry which was probably an attitude of the time.

He was very supportive of aspiring athletes however humble their aims and got on with people from all walks of life, always having a fondness for the people of New Zealand and Australia in particular, where he had many friends. He encouraged me to go to New Zealand on leaving school to study agriculture, for which I have always been grateful.

I have often been asked how it felt to row in the shadow of such a famous father. Well, it didn't worry me at all, as I grew up without fully appreciating what he had achieved. He was very modest in that respect and it was at a time before sportsmen were the celebrities they are today. He didn't enter the public limelight until after his death. The year 2000, after Steve Redgrave won his fifth gold medal and was knighted was perhaps a turning point and he still polls well amongst top British sportsmen and women.

I well remember how quick he was in a sculling boat well into his 60s. It wasn't until I first rowed in the 1st VIII at Bedford School in 1963 that I could beat him on the river at Henley, where we used to scull together and where he had taught me to scull as a young boy.

His letters show that he had a love for the countryside and nature. As a child he used to collect and blow birds eggs and create displays of moths and butterflies, not something that would be approved of now, but it was a common hobby at the time. Later in life beagling every week gave him a great deal of pleasure and kept him fit.

The Olympic Diploma of Merit, Jack Beresford. 1948

Jack's contribution to rowing was recognised with honours in the 1940s. In 1947 Beresford Road near The Embankment was named by Bedford Borough Council in honour of Jack's rowing achievements. In that year he was also awarded the Gold Medal of the International Rowing Federation and in 1948 he received the Olympic Diploma of Merit.

Jack Beresford was appointed CBE in 1960 for his services to rowing which was the year that his nephew, Michael Beresford, competed in the coxless fours in the Rome Olympics. This meant that the Beresford's became the first British family to have three generations represent them at the Olympic Games.

Beagling, Jack Beresford. 1970s

He was rowing correspondent of "The Field" 1966-71, so continuing a long and important connection between that journal and rowing. He also involved himself in the production of some of the first plastic sculling boats.

His life held many interests and activities until his death. He became a Freeman of the City of London in 1952 and was a Master of the Worshipful Company of Furniture Makers.

Veteran Scullers Head of the River Race, Jack Beresford training. Late 1960s

He played the part of the umpire in the musical film version of H.G Wells novel based on "Kipps: The Story of a Simple Soul", called *"Half a Sixpence"* which starred Tommy Steele as Kipps. He was made up as an Edwardian gentleman complete with fine moustaches and rather bizarrely this image was used to depict him for the 1992 BBC *"Tales of Gold"* series, referred to later.

He greatly enjoyed beagling regularly with the Christchurch and Farley Hill Beagles for many years and competed in the Veteran Head of the River Race on the tideway, for which he had trained with characteristic enthusiasm.

A tragic accident happened when aged 70 in 1969 at the National Schools Regatta at Pangbourne, which troubled him for the rest of his life. He was umpiring a race when a boy caught a crab, was swept overboard and being unable to swim was drowning. Umpires' launches are designed for speed not manoeuvrability and could not approach him. Jack, a strong swimmer, dived overboard but when the boy clung to him he could not swim both of them to the surface with the weed and current. The boy died and Jack was very shocked and exhausted. He already had angina and he then suffered a number of other health issues, which may have been triggered by this incident.

He continued to scull on the Thames at Henley almost until the eve of his death. He died at Shiplake on 3rd December 1977, aged 78, the morning after presiding in his own characteristically cheerful manner at the annual dinner of Thames Rowing Club.

The Bishop of London officiated at his Memorial Service held in St. Paul's Cathedral. At this the piper, Major D Duncan of the London Scottish played the regimental march of the Liverpool Scottish. Brigadier H S Hopkinson who gave the address recalled how the young Jack Beresford was badly wounded in the trenches - "*his youthful years in France modelled his next 62*". Suitably enough, Jack had the last word. Some lines inscribed in his beagling book, "*I was glad to be alive because I heard the cry of hounds*", were read by his son John followed by his own epitaph written beneath them: "*Rowing gave me my fitness and strength: Beagling, my wife and happiness*".

A number of racing boats have been named after him, including in 1964 "*50 Plus*" the Bedford School 1st VIII in memory of the more than fifty years between his and his son John being Captain of Boats. This boat had a revolutionary rudder cum fin and although difficult to sit, proved a fast boat, winning the Senior Junior VIIIs at Bedford Regatta in 1964 in record time. On 29th April 2007 "*Jack Beresford*" was named by John Beresford at Thames Rowing Club. This is a women's Empacher pair, which has recently been refurbished and is still being used by Thames senior women's squad for pairs seat racing.

As well as in the 1992 BBC "*Tales of Gold*" series, Beresford featured in an ITV programme "*Britain's Greatest Gold Medalists*" shown just before the London Olympics in 2012. He was recorded as being the first of only five British Olympic medalists who have won medals of any colour in five consecutive Games. The others being: Steve Redgrave (rowing), Katherine Grainger (rowing), Ben Ainslie (sailing) and Bradley Wiggins (cycling).

His Olympic and most other medals can be seen in the Olympic display at the River and Rowing Museum in Henley-on-Thames where they are on loan from the Beresford family.

The Beresford Family. Henley-on-Thames 16ᵗʰ September 1950.
Three generations 1868–1950.

J "Berry" Beresford   Jack Beresford   Eric Beresford   Michael Beresford
Born 1868   Born 1899   Born 1905   Born 1934

John Beresford
Born 1945

Afloat at Henley-On-Thames. 16ᵗʰ September 1950

List of Illustrations by page number

Acknowledgements

I am hugely grateful to the many people who have made it possible for me to produce this book and I apologise if I have not named anyone.

John Jenkins's article "Rowing's Loss – Rugby's Gain" gave a great deal of information about my father's military training and action as well as providing the framework of his rowing achievements and life, which I have expanded to produce this tribute to my father. I thank him for giving me the inspiration to write this book.

Michael Orr provided valuable information for the John Jenkins article, as did the Liverpool Scottish Museum Trust, both of whom I want to thank.

Writer Sophie Livingston gave me much encouragement to produce this book and has been tireless in both editing and structuring the book. Without her efforts I could not have published this.

My family have given me encouragement, photographs and financial support to produce a book which will be of lasting importance for our family's history. More specifically I thank: my wife Jane who also helped with editing and daughter Emma, my sisters Libby Milling, Carina and Pandora and my nephews David and Charles Elliott. David deserves particular thanks for compiling the book into printable format and for final editing.

The following have provided me with material, photographs and support for which I am most grateful:

Diana and Richard Way in Henley-on-Thames.
Chris Dodd, Vice president and Emeritus Historian of Henley River and Rowing Museum.
'Hear the Boat Sing'(HTBS) and Tim Koch, Rowing Historian who writes and researches for *heartheboatsing.com*.
The River and Rowing Museum, Henley-on-Thames.
Thomas E Weil, Collector, with a wealth of rowing memorabilia.

Choir Press in Gloucester have given me much friendly assistance and advice on publishing and marketing this book and whom I highly recommend.

Lightning Source UK Ltd.
Milton Keynes UK
UKHW020400110120
356729UK00003B/7/P